Building Physics of the Envelope

Principles of Construction

The following titles have been published in this series:

Ulrich Knaack, Tillmann Klein, Marcel Bilow, Thomas Auer
Façades – Principles of Construction
Second and revised edition
ISBN 978-3-03821-044-3

Maarten Meijs, Ulrich Knaack, Tillmann Klein
Components and Connections in Architecture – Principles of Construction
ISBN 978-3-7643-8669-6

Ulrich Knaack, Sharon Chung-Klatte, Reinhard Hasselbach
Prefabricated Systems – Principles of Construction
ISBN 978-3-7643-8747-1

ULRICH KNAACK
EDDIE KOENDERS (EDS.)

ELENA ALEXANDRAKIS
DAVID BEWERSDORFF
INES HAAKE
SASCHA HICKERT
CHRISTOPH MANKEL

Building Physics of the Envelope

Principles of Construction

BIRKHÄUSER

BASEL

We would like to thank Technische Universität Darmstadt for the financial support of this publication. We would also like to thank Ria Stein for her editorial guidance and Claudia Siegele for her subject editing. Thanks are due to the students Barbara Bauer, Sina Aghababaei Najjar and Jacqueline Sienell who created the drawings. Finally we are grateful to Prof. Dr. Normen Langner for his valuable contribution to the content and for his support.

Layout and cover design: Nicole Schwarz, Typolabor, Berlin
Graphic concept 'Principles of Construction' series: Oliver Kleinschmidt, Berlin

Authors of the individual chapters:
1 Introduction – Ulrich Knaack, Eddie Koenders
2 Thermal Energy – Christoph Mankel
3 Moisture – Elena Alexandrakis, David Bewersdorff
4 Airtightness – David Bewersdorff
5 Acoustics – Ines Haake
6 Light – Sascha Hickert
7 Building Physics in Practice – David Bewersdorff, Sascha Hickert, Ulrich Knaack
8 Building Physics and Materials – Eddie Koenders
9 Building Physics and the Building Envelope – Ulrich Knaack

Subject editor: Claudia Siegele, bausatz, Karlsruhe
Editor: Ria Stein, Berlin
Translation into English: Usch Engelmann, Rotterdam
Production: Amelie Solbrig, Berlin
Paper: Magno Satin, 150 g/qm
Lithography: [bildpunkt] Druckvorstufen GmbH, Berlin
Printing: optimal media GmbH, Röbel
Cover photograph: Ed White (Wood Innovation and Design Centre, MGA | Michael Green Architecture, Prince George, 2014)

This publication is also available as an e-book (ISBN 978-3-0356-0949-3) and a German language edition (ISBN 978-3-0356-1134-2).

Library of Congress Control Number: 2018940683

Bibliographic information published by the German National Library
The German National Library lists this publication in the Deutsche Nationalbibliografie; detailed bibliographic data are available on the Internet at http://dnb.dnb.de.

© 2018 Birkhäuser Verlag GmbH, Basel
P.O. Box 44, 4009 Basel, Switzerland
Part of Walter de Gruyter GmbH, Berlin/Boston
Printed on acid-free paper produced from chlorine-free pulp. TCF ∞
Printed in Germany

ISBN 978-3-0356-1145-8

9 8 7 6 5 4 3 2 1
www.birkhauser.com

Contents

1
Introduction

WHY BUILDING PHYSICS?

The physical aspects of and in buildings need to be considered in the early planning stages. An example: as a consequence of the fact that a residential building project in Berlin during the Wilhelminian era (the so-called Gründerjahre, beginning around 1870) was predominantly commercially driven, the flats were organised in such a compact manner that it was only the turn radius of the firefighting equipment that defined the dimensions of the courtyard – 5.34 × 5.34 m. With the result that the flats were insufficiently ventilated; harming the occupants and, at a later stage, the building itself since insufficient ventilation and deficient heating systems caused excessive humidity. Simple, minimal ventilation measures remedied the situation – and illustrated the relevance of the physical conditions in buildings. One consequence of the oil crisis of 1973 was that the energy consumption of buildings became a significant aspect in planning: better insulation, more efficient heating and cooling systems as well as an energetically optimised orientation of the building. However, besides energy savings, the general well-being of building occupants is a major goal in planning and realising buildings – and it is here that the topic building physics starts to develop. Building physics deals with transition and transmission phenomena within a construction and between materials. Critical aspects hereby are thermal energy, moisture, airtightness (or air permeability), acoustics and light. Areas of research and evaluation are energy transport as well as the transformation processes and their impact on the construction element itself and the adjacent areas on the inside and the outside. With building physics, the processes can be explained, and predictions can be made about the expectable performance of constructions. However, not only the result of the individual process is interesting but also the interrelation between the different phenomena; for example, water condensation on cold surfaces such as non-insulated massive walls as a result of the temperature-dependent water absorption capacity of air – with the risk of mould growth or frost damage.

Next to these technical aspects, the occupants' comfort level is an important topic; meaning a person's sense of physical and psychological well-being. Since this is a subjective sensation, basic verification of individual technical aspects is insufficient to conduct a complete evaluation. It is important to link the individual phenomena with each other and to consciously accept subjective assessments; it will not be possible to generate the optimal room climate for everybody at all times, but the goal will be reached if 80% of the occupants are generally satisfied.

THERMAL ENERGY, MOISTURE, AIRTIGHTNESS, SOUND AND LIGHT

Building physics is categorised in thermal energy or temperature, moisture, airtightness, acoustics or sound and light, even though strong links exist between these fields. The category thermal energy deals with the development and the transport of heat through the air and through construction elements. This includes the physical phenomena of heat transfer from one medium to another and of different aggregate states, especially of water. Another aspect is the effect of the phenomena on the human being and its sense of well-being. The category moisture or humidity deals with air-bound water besides constructional aspects related to humidity in and on the building. Of particular interest are water absorption and discharge of the air at different temperatures and the resulting consequences for a construction, such as condensation on cold surfaces.

The phenomena thermal energy and moisture are also directly influenced by airtightness. Non-tight constructions facilitate heat exchange as well as penetration of humidity. Thus, constructions should be protected accordingly or equipped with ventilation facilities.

The category sound and acoustics is treated somewhat differently than thermal energy and moisture. It deals with the propagation of sound as an energy impulse in the air (airborne sound) or in construction elements (solid-borne sound). Based hereupon, the planning phase must include the decision whether construction elements should be realised in a flexible or massive manner in order to minimise sound propagation. An aspect that goes beyond the scope of this book is the targeted control of sound to achieve acoustic effects.

Light is important to enable the use of a building – be it in the form of natural light from the outside or artificial light. In addition, this category deals with the necessity of a direct relation of the building with the exterior and a reduction of solar energy input by means of shading.

Effects on the human being

As human beings we stand in continuous reciprocal action with the building we are in. It is therefore important to understand and control the building physics behaviour of the building and its effects on the human being. Façades and their materials determine our environment and the user comfort. The chosen geometries of the façades together with the materials used have a significant effect on the reciprocation between human and building.

Our sense of well-being is subjective. It is possible that in a specific building one person feels very comfortable because temperature and humidity are sensed as balanced, and that another person feels very uncomfortable in the same building because he/she feels very hot following a sporting activity. It is the task of building physics to organise these environmental conditions of the building such that, on average, about 80 % of the occupants are satisfied.

The reciprocation between human and building encompasses a sensitive balance of the building physics influences such as thermal energy, moisture, airtightness, sound and light. Even small changes of these influences can alter a situation from pleasant to unpleasant. A small change in temperature, for example, can make our body begin to release energy to the environment in order to reestablish the balance. The body temperature falls, and we experience the environment as too cold. The equivalent is valid for the other influences such as humidity; for example: the body starts to transpire if the humidity in the room is too high. It is therefore important to consider the balance of the building physics influences and to optimise them in their entirety; so that the human being feels comfortable under any circumstance.

FAÇADE MATERIAL AND CONSTRUCTION AS STORAGE AND BARRIER

The material used in a building needs to meet building physics requirements in addition to the constructional functions it serves. The requirements posed on buildings have risen continuously over the past decade. And the discussion about climate change has further influenced our awareness and understanding of well-being in buildings. Therefore, material and construction have evolved together in their mutual dependency. They offer the opportunity to influence our environment and therefore our sense of well-being with integral solutions.

Increasingly, modern developments in the field of building physics are oriented toward the energy efficiency of the overall building. Hereby, façade and material are viewed as energy-active parts of the building. Excess heat is dissipated to the environment via walls and façades, or stored in walls → 1. Modern material development makes this form of energy storage possible and results in the fact that the building can be viewed as an energy-active element, and not merely as shell and construction; heat storage in material or construction elements is already being applied in prototypes. Heat storage in phase change materials (PCM), for example, can take place in gypsum boards to control the temperature inside spaces and, thus, to save energy. In this manner, building physics, materials and constructions are energetically optimised in integral solutions. Additional developments in this field lead to new integrated material and construction concepts such as gradient concretes, for example, that specifically exploit the heat storage and barrier properties of concrete → 2. This opens up a whole new world of possibilities that reveal new and innovative solutions in the field of building physics as the interface between material and construction.

1

Research project ETA-Fabrik, Darmstadt Technical University, 2016
This energy-efficient experimental building comprises of an exterior façade that absorbs solar energy (heat) and transfers it into a storage system. When necessary, the energy is dissipated into the interior space. If cooling is required, this principle can be inversed.

2

Heat-insulating concrete
Mineralised foam with density values below 200 kg/m³ can be used as heat insulation. Its pore content lies at approximately 90 %, its solids matrix typically consists of cement stone and additives.

3

Unilever House, Hamburg, Behnisch Architekten, 2009
The double façade consists of an inner glass layer and an outer
foil façade. The air space between the layers serves to climati-
cally condition the office spaces.

4

Office building Manitoba Hydro Place, Winnipeg, KPMB Architects, 2009
The office building is ventilated by means of thermal lift created in the solar chimney. The chimney
creates a suction that introduces fresh air into the building (climate concept: Transsolar).

BUILDING ENVELOPE AS
BARRIER BETWEEN INTERIOR AND EXTERIOR

The building envelope is the barrier between the interior and the exterior – the place where the energy flow is interrupted or deflected. Accordingly, the building envelope exercises a direct and significant influence on the interior space and its functionality as well as on the energy balance of the building. Depending on the construction, joints and materials used, energy flows and humidity transport are inhibited, limited or enabled, if so desired. Good insulating properties allow keeping heat inside the building in winter, and to exclude it in summer → 3. Materials/constructions with these properties are usually light, exhibit little heat conduction, and are thus typically not suited for load-bearing constructions. In contrast, massive constructions cannot only fulfil the loadbearing function but, as good heat conductors, they are also able to store thermal energy, and thus, to store and dissipate heat over the course of the day, balancing out temperature differences. This contrariness needs to be considered and exploited when deciding for a certain building envelope so that the necessary advantages of a certain function are optimised; in the mentioned example this is achieved with a heavy, loadbearing construction on the inside that is insulated with a light, non-loadbearing material on the outside. Of course, the decisions need to take the local climate and the function of the building into account.

The constructions shown in this book are typical technical solutions, based on systems that are broadly applied in practice. Strategies have been selected in each of the categories thermal energy, moisture, airtightness, sound and light that offer optimal technical and economic solutions for the construction. Since, as mentioned before, there is always the need to weigh the individual building physics requirements and the according solutions, not all demands are always completely solvable and constructive compromises are identified.

Climate design as a tool for better buildings

Climate design or climate engineering involves a combination of the components of the building relevant for building physics, the materials and the building envelope itself → 4. This relatively new planning discipline deals with the direct dependency of bio-physical phenomena of the building volume, the dimensions (materials) of the building, the building envelope (construction, share of transparent areas), the building orientation as well as the function-based energy sources and the qualities necessary for the well-being of the user. The integral consideration of all of these parameters and optimisation of individual aspects allow for increased efficiency, not only in terms of functionality but also of improved energy consumption.

Other developments with regard to building improvement concern the aspect of embodied energy, i.e. the energy needed to produce the materials used: here, the ratio of the energy needed to produce materials and constructions and the energy to be saved during the building's life span is decisive during planning.

Similarly, evolving concepts that involve adapting the material- and construction-related parameters seem promising. Building envelopes that consist of switchable materials which, based on actual need and energy balance, can absorb, store and dissipate heat, offer the possibility to balance out the day and night cycles, and thus contribute to the overall energy balance of the building. Economically, this could be called 'building physics 4.0', whereby integral solutions do not only include construction planning but also energy saving potential through thermal storage, possible use of bio-based solutions and exploitation of reusing natural resources, all based on modern, digital production technologies. Great challenges lie ahead – while the building industry will also face large investments in knowledge and modern technologies.

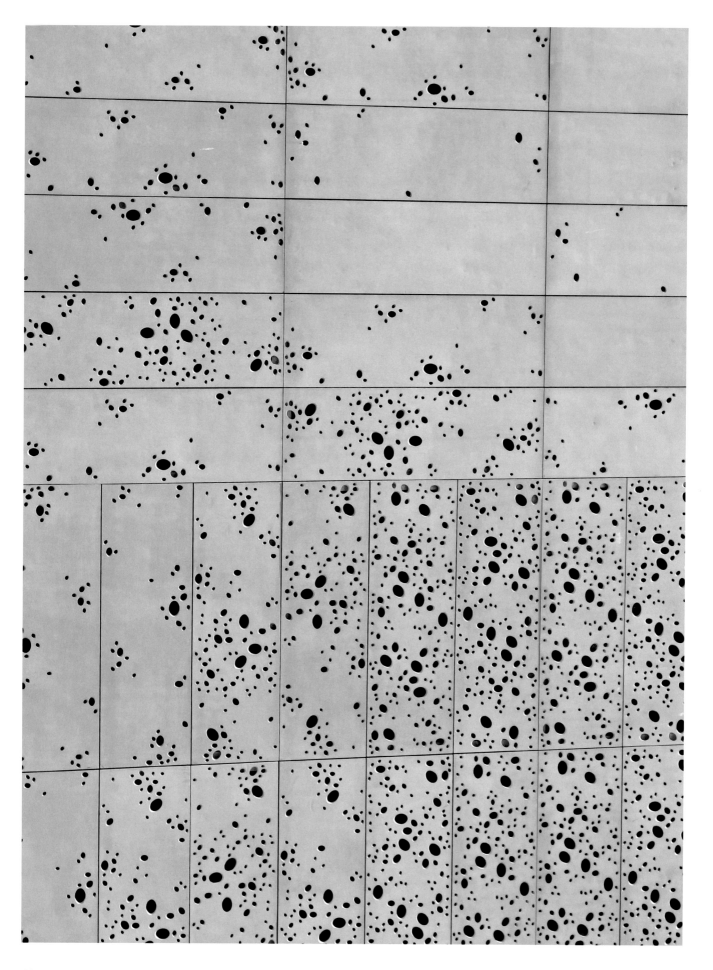

2

Thermal Energy

For the human being, heat or thermal energy is an easily understandable physical phenomenon. Amongst other things this is because temperature as a linear measurement of this energy can easily be sensed by our body. We feel heat directly with our largest organ, the skin, and can well differentiate between low temperatures in winter and high temperatures in summer. From a physical point of view, heat is a form of energy that results from the kinetic energy of atoms and molecules of matter.

In the building industry, thermal energy plays an important role. The goal is to achieve a thermally comfortable and hygienic room climate for the human being. During winter, indoor spaces might need to be heated, while cooled during summer. This must be done with as little energy expenditure as possible. It is also mandatory to avoid condensation on construction element surfaces at all cost to eliminate the risk of mould growth. Thus, a building envelope must comply with a certain insulation standard. Planning of these measures requires fundamental knowledge in the field of thermodynamics.

COMFORT

The sense of comfort or well-being of a person contributes significantly to the person's health and productivity. Within a building, the room climate is the decisive factor. Room temperature and relative humidity must be adjusted depending on the clothing and activities of the occupants. But factors such as the temperature of the construction element surfaces and the velocity of the air also affect the sense of well-being of the occupants, who, in addition, each have individual perceptions concerning the indoor climate. Thus, comfort is not an exact but rather a subjective parameter.

Reference values are regulated by the so-called 'acceptable room climate' as the basis for evaluation. According to DIN EN ISO 7730, 80% of empirically generated data sets must rate the room climate as thermally comfortable. A comfortable sensation is achieved if a balance between the heat output generated by the body and the heat flow dissipated from the body is created with the lowest possible effort. The heat dissipated from the body depends on the ambient temperature, the activity and the clothing. The point of reference is a person with a weight of 80 kg. At 20 °C, the heat dissipation or the heat flow is around 100 W in a resting position (sitting).

The heat flow dissipating from the body is composed of the convective heat output into the air and the radiative heat output onto surrounding surfaces. The larger the temperature difference between the body temperature and the room temperature or the temperature of the space-enclosing surfaces, the greater is the resulting heat flow. This interrelation has a negative effect on our sense of comfort. This effect is particularly noticeable when a person is situated near a cold construction element surface in winter; for example, a large window. The heat flow between the body surface and the construction element surface can become so great that it creates an unpleasant draught sensation on the skin. Increasing the temperature of the wall surface immediately improves the sense of comfort.

Additionally, the relationship between temperature and relative humidity is of great importance. At temperatures around 21 °C (± 2 °C), relative humidity can vary between 35% and 70%, and is typically perceived as comfortable in spite of this significant range. Higher temperatures and/or rising relative humidity create a sense of sultry mugginess. High humidity levels inhibit the body's own temperature regulation because sweating means that the body can no longer dissipate enough energy by the effect of evaporative cooling. Low temperatures combined with high relative humidity are perceived as uncomfortably wet and cold. Hereby, the body loses heat due to the higher heat conductivity of the air, and the resulting evaporative cooling on the skin surface cools the body even further.

HEAT TRANSMISSION

Heat is a form of energy with temperature being the state variable. Temperature is the measurement of the kinetic energies of particles within a material or material system. This is true for the oscillation energy of the molecules of solid matter as well as for the random movement of molecules of gases and fluids.

The transport of thermal energy is principally bound to a temperature difference within a material. Hereby, heat is always transported from high temperature levels toward lower temperature levels. The resulting heat flow describes the quantity of heat transported per time unit. With reference to a transport surface, the result is the heat flux density. The most important heat transmission mechanisms of thermodynamics are heat conduction, convection and radiation.

Heat conduction

Heat conduction describes the principal heat transport mechanism in solid materials and material systems that contact each other. Every atom of a material oscillates around its resting position within an oscillation radius depending on the temperature. The resting position is the atom's position at 0°Kelvin = −273,15 °Celsius (absolute zero). If an atom is in its resting position, it does not exert any kinetic energy. Oscillation energy occurs at rising temperatures.

Depending on the structural conditions of a material or material system, its atoms are arranged in molecular structures, atomic structures or mixed structures. The denser the atoms and molecules are packed, the more frequently their oscillation radii overlap and the higher is the probability that they collide during oscillation. The collisions cause thermal energy to be transmitted from strongly oscillating atoms and molecules to adjacent lesser oscillating ones, and to be conducted through the material system. The material model → 1 illustrates the probability of potential collisions depending on the material structure.

The material-specific unit to describe a material's thermic conductivity properties is thermic conductivity λ [W/m·K]. Thermic conductivity determines how much thermal energy is transported per unit of length of a material layer and a temperature delta of 1 Kelvin. Thermic conductivity is influenced by the factors density, moisture content and temperature. Materials with dense atom and molecule packing (high density) therefore exhibit high thermic conductivity whereas the thermic conductivity of materials with low density packing is low.

Additionally, thermic conductivity increases with increasing moisture. This effect results from embedded water molecules within the pore structure of a material that act as contact bridges between the molecular structure and therefore facilitate the transport of energy. Owing to the increasing kinetic energy, thermic conductivity of dense as well as porous materials typically increases at rising temperatures. This effect is more prominent with porous materials such as insulating materials, for example.

The general heat conduction equation according to Fourier's law describes the phenomenon of thermic conductivity through a layer of material in a one-dimensional case → 2.

$$\rho c \, \frac{\partial T}{\partial t} = \lambda \, \frac{\partial^2 T}{\partial x^2}$$

with λ Thermic conductivity [W/mK]
      ρ Density [kg/m³]
      c Specific heat capacity [J/kgK]

Material with low raw density

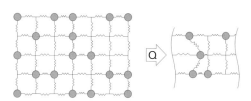

Material with high raw density

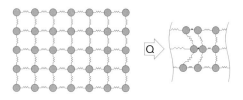

1

Thermal conductivity depending on the material's raw density
The material model shows the atoms or molecules connected by a spring system as well as their vibrational behaviour depending on the material structure. The denser a compound structure, the greater the possibility of potential contact. In a simplified manner the model only shows the vibrational movements in horizontal direction. The true molecular movement and heat transmission takes place in a three-dimensional space.

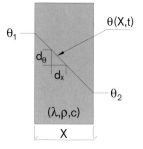

2

Heat conduction equation according to Fourier's law
The heat conduction equation describes the material-specific, non-stationary temperature distribution across a material section depending on the material's layer thickness and time.

Usually, non-stationary boundary conditions prevail in nature. How temperature is distributed across a cross-section and how long the distribution takes depends on the thermic conductivity and the thermic storage capacity of the material. The coefficient of thermic conductivity formulates these effects.

$$\alpha = \frac{\lambda}{\rho \cdot c}$$

It describes the speed with which a temperature wave is transmitted through a material with a 1 m² area, i.e. how fast a certain material reacts to temperature changes.

This book presupposes stationary conditions; with the consequence of time-independent boundary conditions and constant temperature distribution.

Convection

Heat transmission through convection occurs when the thermal energy of a body is transmitted to a passing medium, such as air, for example, or conversely, when the thermal energy of a passing medium is transmitted to a body. When a heat source heats up air molecules, they start to move. The volume of the heated air increases, and its density decreases. The warm air rises, thereby cooling continuously. During cooling, the volume decreases, so that the cold air sinks while its density increases. This process causes a continuous reciprocal flow.

If the warm air molecules pass along the cold surface of a body, the thermal energy is transmitted to the surface of the body. Analogously, warm body surfaces can transfer thermal energy to adjacent air molecules, which in turn creates a flow. This process based on different densities is called convection. Contrary to free convection, convection flows can also be artificially generated with an air flow source such as a fan or wind. This type of convection is called 'forced convection'.

The resulting heat flux density q between a body and an adjacent gaseous or liquid medium depends on the temperature of the flowing medium θ_U and the body surface temperature θ_S. In addition, a body's surface roughness and the velocity of the flowing medium strongly influence the heat transmission. Both of these influencing parameters are considered in the heat transmission coefficient h_v.

The convective heat flux density q is generated by the multiplication of the heat transmission coefficient h_v with the prevailing temperature difference between the flowing medium θ_U and the body surface temperature θ_S. The greater the temperature difference and the heat transmission coefficient, the greater the resulting heat flow and the better the heat transmission → **3**.

$$q = h_v (\theta_s - \theta_u)$$

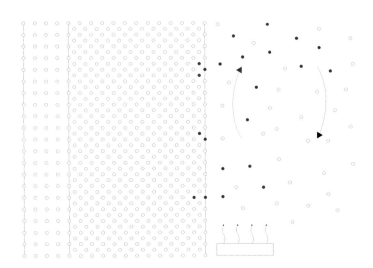

3

Heat transmission through convection
The graph shows a convection flow caused by a heat and/or air flow source. Warm air with low density (red) rises and cold air with higher density (black) sinks. The heated air molecules flow along a cold wall surface and transfer their thermal energy. Cooled air molecules sink back down so that a reciprocal convection flow occurs.

Heat transmission by radiation

Radiation energy is created by the atoms or molecules of a material moving and being transmitted in the form of electromagnetic waves. The stronger the kinetic energy of the atoms or molecules of a material, the greater the radiation energy emitting from it. In physics, a material that either receives or transmits radiation energy is called emitter. The total energy of an emitter consists of short-wave, visible light energy (wavelength 0–3000 nm) and long-wave infrared radiation (wavelength between 3000 nm and 800 μm). With rising temperatures, the radiation's wavelength shifts according to Wien's displacement law to increasingly short lengths.

If, for example, energy is supplied to an iron rod, the rod heats up and initially transmits invisible thermal radiation via infrared radiation. If the rod is heated further, it begins to glow red. Now, a part short-wave visible radiation adds on to the invisible radiation. With further heating, the share of short-wave visible radiation increases until the rod glows whitely.

The entire energy transmission of radiation E is composed of the parts reflection ρ, absorption α, transmission τ and emission ε. The parts of radiation can be illustrated in an overall balance → **4**.

Incident energy $E_E = E_\rho + E_\alpha + E_\tau$ ($\rho + \alpha + \tau = 1$)
Emitting energy $E_A = E_\rho + E_\varepsilon + E_\tau$ ($\rho + \varepsilon + \tau = 1$)

If energy is only transported by radiation, temperature constancy exists for $E_E = E_A$. For $E_E \neq E_A$ a difference remains that causes heating of the material if $E_E > E_A$, and cooling of the material if $E_E < E_A$. Heat transmission through a body is based on thermal conductance. In simple terms, heat transmission by radiation can be viewed as a surface phenomenon.

The so-called black radiator is defined as an ideal radiator. It simultaneously absorbs and emits all radiation energy; transmission and reflection are excluded. Hereby, its properties are material-independent and are only defined by its temperature. Depending on the temperature, coloured surfaces can also function as a black radiator. In physical terms, our sun, for example, is a black radiator, in spite of its white-yellowish appearance. The relevant material surfaces in the building industry act as so-called grey bodies.

Energy emission and energy absorption of grey bodies are reduced by their degree of emission ε and degree of absorption α, which determine the relationship between the energy density of the grey body and a black radiator. According to Kirchhoff (Kirchhoff's law of thermal radiation), degree of emission and degree of absorption are equal $\varepsilon = \alpha$.

Kirchhoff's law cannot be applied to solar radiation as it has relatively short wavelengths. The emission and absorption behaviour of materials is different for long- and short-wave radiation; therefore $\varepsilon \neq \alpha$.

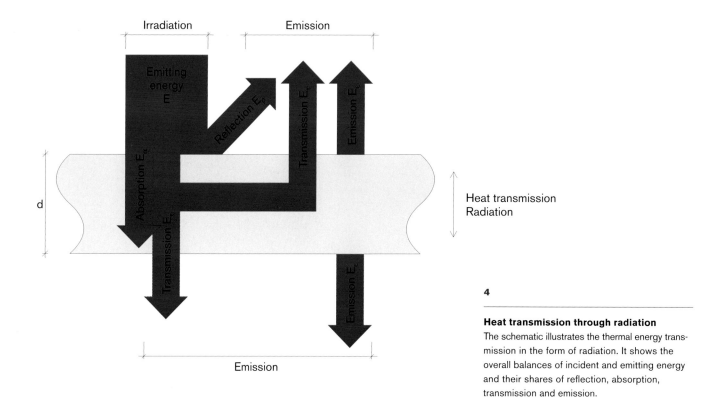

4

Heat transmission through radiation
The schematic illustrates the thermal energy transmission in the form of radiation. It shows the overall balances of incident and emitting energy and their shares of reflection, absorption, transmission and emission.

Energy transmission between bodies, surfaces and volumes via electromagnetic waves requires a temperature gradient to create energy flow. Heat exchange occurs from higher temperature to lower temperature, and is not bound to a medium; i.e. thermal radiation can also transmit heat in a vacuum. The process depends on the temperature (temperature distribution), the optical properties and the surface geometry.

THERMAL BOUNDARY RESISTANCE

Heat transfer describes the thermal energy exchange between a gas and the surface of a solid medium. The heat transfer in this boundary surface area is predominantly determined by the two thermal transmission mechanisms radiation and convection. Air exhibits very little thermal conductivity, making this share of thermal conductance negligible.

The phenomenon of heat transfer is described with the heat transfer coefficient h or the thermal boundary resistance R_S. The heat transfer coefficient is a combination of the two heat transfer coefficients h_r (radiation) and h_v (convection). It describes the amount of thermal energy that is transmitted per second at a temperature delta of 1 Kelvin at the boundary surface of a solid medium of 1 m². The larger the value of the particular heat transfer coefficient or the smaller the thermal boundary resistance, the more thermal energy can be transmitted per time unit and temperature change. In this context, the radiation-caused transmission coefficient h_r rises in proportion to an increase in temperature of the ambient air on the surface of the solid medium and its degree of emission. The value of the convective transmission coefficient h_v is determined by the flow rate of the gas (air) present in the boundary surface area of a gas/solid medium. With high flow rates, many free gas molecules flow along the molecular structure of the surface of the solid medium, resulting in a good thermal energy exchange in the boundary surface area.

The heat transfer coefficient h is the sum of the radiation-caused heat transfer coefficient h_r and the convective transfer coefficient h_v. The thermal boundary resistance R_S is formed with the reciprocal value of the heat transfer coefficient h.

In the building industry, the thermal boundary resistance is defined via the direction of the heat flow. Hereby, there is a differentiation between inside, outside, upward, horizontal and downward. Different resistances occur; particularly in the inner area. Overall, the interior thermal boundary resistance R_{si} increases from an upward-oriented heat flow toward a downward-oriented heat flow. This is mainly due to free convective processes. Warm air rises and cold air sinks.

Thermal boundary resistances of constructions that border on outside air (R_{se}) are predominantly influenced by forced convective flows of the exterior air. Building part specific values for the inner and outer heat transmission resistance can be found in the building norms and standards.

THERMAL CAPACITY

Simply said, thermal capacity describes the property of a material to absorb thermal energy and to emit it during cooling. The thermal capacity of a construction mainly depends on the thermal properties of the materials used. Massive construction elements, in particular, can store large amounts of thermal energy. In this context, raw density ρ and specific thermal capacity c_{spec} are decisive parameters to describe a material's thermal storage capacity.

The specific thermal capacity indicates the amount of energy needed to heat a material by 1°Kelvin. Supplying heat or activity increases the interior energy of a material. The thermal energy supplied to a material is stored in the form of internal energy. The storage occurs in translational, rotational and vibrational degrees of freedom of the molecules. Each particle requires energy to be excited to translation, rotation and/or vibration, depending on its degrees of freedom. In simple terms, and sufficiently precise for building construction purposes, solid matter can only be excited to vibrate. Thus, it can be derived that the more particles per mass unit of a material are present, the more energy (E) is required to induce vibration → **5**.

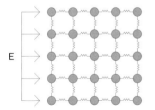 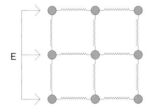

5

Particle density per mass unit of a material
A material comprises a certain number of particles per mass unit (e.g. per gram). The more particles per gram of material, the more energy is required to excite them into vibration, and the greater the specific heat capacity of this material. The illustration on the left shows a high specific heat capacity while the one on the right illustrates a low heat capacity.

The larger the specific thermal capacity and the raw density, the more thermal energy can be stored during a temperature change and the longer it takes for a material to heat or cool → **6**. This type of heat storage is called sensible heat storage. The following equation describes the storable thermal energy Q:

$$Q = c_{spez} \cdot \rho \cdot V \cdot \Delta\theta$$

with c_{spez} Specific thermal capacity [Wh/(kgK)]
ρ Raw density [kg/m³]
V Volume [m³]
$\Delta\theta$ Temperature difference [K]

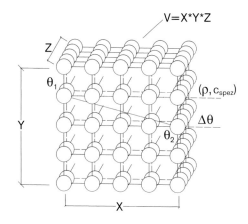

6

Storable thermal energy of a material
The storable thermal energy of a solid material results from the product of the specific heat capacity, raw density, the volume and a prevailing temperature difference. This connection is illustrated in this schematic structure.

HEAT TRANSFER THROUGH CONSTRUCTION ELEMENTS

In the building industry, the term heat transfer means the transport of thermal energy through a construction element, whereby this process is influenced by interior and exterior climate boundary conditions. It considers the heat transport within material-specific construction element layers and the particular heat transfer between the inner surface of the construction element and the interior environment as well as the exterior surface of the construction element and the exterior environment.

Heat transmission resistance of opaque construction elements

Opaque construction elements consist of non-transparent material layers. The heat transmission resistance R of such a homogenous construction element layer describes the resistance against thermal energy conduction through the material of a specific layer → **7**. Thus, the thermal resistance is the coefficient of layer thickness d and thermal conductivity λ of the material of the construction element layer.

$$R = \frac{d}{\lambda} \ [m^2 K/W]$$

7

Heat transmission resistance
The heat transmission resistance describes the material-specific resistance that opposes the transmission of thermal energy through heat conduction. It is calculated from the coefficient of the material layer thickness and the thermal conductivity. The greater the material thickness and the smaller the thermal conductivity, the greater is the heat transmission resistance.

For construction elements consisting of several material layers, heat transmission resistance is calculated by adding up the individual resistances → **8**.

$$R = \sum_{i=1}^{n} \frac{d_i}{\lambda_i} \ [m^2 K/W]$$

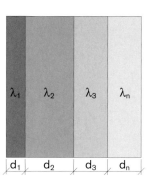

8

Heat transmission resistance of multiple material layers
The heat transmission resistance of composed material layers is calculated from the addition of the individual resistances of each of the material layers.

Thermal resistance of air layers

Within air layers, heat transfer takes place via thermal conduction, convection and radiation. Hereby, thermal conduction accounts for the smallest share. Different thermal resistances (heat transmission resistance) result from variations in the air flow rate and the thickness of the air layer. The building industry differentiates between static and lightly or strongly ventilated air layers.

The heat transmission resistance of static air layers initially rises with increasing layer thickness. Depending on the thickness of the layer, a free convection flow occurs that, next to a small share of radiation and conductance, becomes increasingly significant. From a layer thickness of 20–25 mm onward, free convection becomes the predominating heat transmission mechanism. The heat transmission resistance does not grow any further with increasing layer thickness, but rather approaches a specific threshold value.

Lightly or strongly ventilated air layers in the façade require ventilation slots to enable the desired air flow. The larger the ventilation slots, the greater the air flow within the air layer. The dominating forced convection heat transfer leads to increased heat outflow so that it can be assumed that with strongly ventilated air layers successive construction element layers no longer have an insulating effect. Rated values for air layers with different ventilation can be found in relevant specialist literature and standard guidelines.

Thermal resistance and heat transmission coefficient

Contrary to the thermal resistance, absolute heat transmission resistance also takes into account the thermal boundary resistance of the boundary layers between a construction element and the inner and outer environment. Absolute heat transmission resistance is calculated as the sum of all individual transmission resistances of the construction element layers and the inner thermal boundary resistance R_{si} as well as the outer thermal boundary resistance R_{se}.

The reciprocal value of the absolute heat transmission resistance R_T forms the heat transmission coefficient or U-value → **9**. In the building industry, the insulating effect of construction elements is calculated with the U-value. The U-value of construction elements with a homogenous layer structure is determined as follows:

$$R_T = \sum_{i=1}^{n} \frac{d_i}{\lambda_i} + R_{si} + R_{se} \; [m^2K/W]$$

$$U = \frac{1}{R_{si} + R_1 + R_2 + ... R_n + R_{se}} = \frac{1}{R_T} \; [m^2K/W]$$

Non-homogenously composed construction elements must be examined in a differentiated manner as not only a one-dimensional heat flow occurs through the construction element in the direction of the layer sequence, but another heat flow orthogonally to the layer sequence. This is due to deviant layer structures, such as different material thicknesses within one layer, for example, or materials with different thermal conductivity. Thus, the two-dimensional influences must be considered when determining the U-value.

When calculating the absolute heat transmission resistance, an upper threshold R_u and a lower threshold R_l are determined that indicate the parallel and orthogonal heat flows. The arithmetic mean of the two thresholds describes the thermal boundary resistance R_T of the non-homogenous construction element.

A detailed calculation of this procedure exceeds the scope of this book. Subsequent aspects are simplified and refer to homogenously structured construction elements.

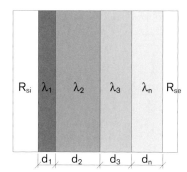

9

Absolute heat transmission resistance und heat transmission coefficient
The absolute heat transmission resistance is calculated from the sum of the individual heat transmission resistances and the addition of the inner and outer thermal boundary resistances. Therefore, this parameter does not only describe the material-specific properties but also the behaviour of a construction element under defined ambient boundary conditions. The U-value is the reciprocal value of the absolute heat transmission resistance. It is the main indicator to evaluate the thermal insulating properties of a construction element.

Stationary temperature gradient within a construction element

In a one-dimensional case, heat flux density q is equal at every point of the construction element → 10, which means it can be formulated generally and for layers j through n, including the boundary layers between construction element surface and interior i as well as construction element surface and exterior e, as follows:

$$q = U \cdot (\theta_i - \theta_e) \qquad \text{General}$$

$$q = q_i = h_i \cdot (\theta_i - \theta_{si}) \qquad \text{Inner heat transfer}$$

$$q = q_j = \frac{\lambda_j}{d_j} \cdot (\theta_{si} - \theta_{j/j+1}) \qquad \text{Layer j}$$

$$q = q_n = \frac{\lambda_n}{d_n} \cdot (\theta_{n-1/n} - \theta_{se}) \qquad \text{Layer n}$$

$$q = q_e = h_e \cdot (\theta_{se} - \theta_e) \qquad \text{Outer heat transfer}$$

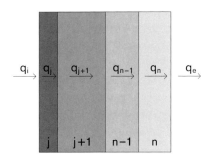

10

Heat flow density in a one-dimensional case
Heat flow density describes how much energy is transmitted through a construction element per time unit and square metre. It is equal in every material layer.

By rearranging the equations in → 10, the temperature gradient can be determined for a one-dimensional heat transmission under stationary boundary conditions of a multi-layer construction element → 11.

$$\theta_{si} = \theta_i - \left(\frac{1}{h_i}\right) \cdot q$$

$$\theta_{j/j+1} = \theta_{si} - \left(\frac{d_j}{\lambda_j}\right) \cdot q$$

$$\theta_{j+1/n-1} = \theta_{j/j+1} - \left(\frac{d_{j+1}}{\lambda_{j+1}}\right) \cdot q$$

$$\theta_{n-1/n} = \theta_{j+1/n-1} - \left(\frac{d_{n-1}}{\lambda_{n-1}}\right) \cdot q$$

$$\theta_{se} = \theta_{n-1/n} - \left(\frac{d_n}{\lambda_n}\right) \cdot q$$

$$\theta_e = \theta_{se} - \left(\frac{1}{h_e}\right) \cdot q$$

HEAT PROTECTION IN SUMMER

One major topic in building physics is the protection from heat in summer, i.e. avoiding high indoor temperature peaks on hot summer days in the most energy-efficient manner possible to create a comfortable room climate.

Maximum acceptable room temperature values are specified for different regions and climate zones so that the impact of specific climatic conditions on a building can be taken into account during planning. The construction as well as measures related to building services are used to minimise the number of hours with temperatures above these maximum values. Hereby, the construction type of a building plays a major role: massive building elements with a high raw density and a high specific heat capacity provide good heat storage. Such building elements heat up slowly, and thereby reduce the increase in room temperature. Other parameters influencing heat protection in summer are room geometry, type and intensity of room ventilation as well as quantity, inclination, energy permeability and shading of the transparent building elements. The manner of shading in particular influences the temperature development inside a room. More detailed information can be found in chapter 6, 'Light', later in this book.

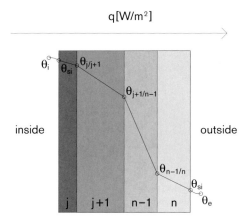

11

Stationary temperature gradation in a one-dimensional case
Temperature gradation across a construction element section results from the linear join of the boundary temperatures between two adjacent construction element layers. The boundary areas in the areas of the inner and the outer heat transfer are part of the equation. The temperature of the following adjacent layers is calculated by subtracting the heat flux density of the product of the individual resistance of a layer multiplied with the heat flux density from the previous temperature.

THERMAL INSULATION IN FOUR EXTERIOR WALL TYPES

The transmission mechanisms of heat were explained at the beginning of this chapter. Now, four typical, practice-oriented wall constructions will illustrate the mechanisms of heat transmission and their advantages and disadvantages in respect to thermal insulation.

An extremely simplified schematic depiction of heat transmission shows the molecular level and the density in the form of scattered points. If the molecules or points lie further apart from each other, the material exhibits low density. Molecules in close proximity to one another mean higher density.

Strictly speaking, porous materials exhibit convection and radiation processes depending on the characteristics of the pores in addition to 'true' thermal conductivity. Thus, thermal conductivity must be viewed as 'effective' thermal conductivity. The following schematic presentation does not consider this phenomenon any further. Heat conduction is simply viewed as contact between adjacent, vibrating molecules. The red circles schematically depict the vibration radii of the individual atoms or molecules around their idle state. The number of circles and their section planes show probability of atoms or molecules colliding. The more section planes, the more molecule collisions are to be expected and the higher is the thermal conductivity of the material shown. The line thickness of the vibration circles is a simplified representation of the temperature gradient.

Single-shell wall construction

The single-shell, loadbearing exterior wall made of reinforced concrete is plastered on the outside surface → **12**. The upper image shows the situation in winter; the lower image that in summer. It is very apparent that the reinforced concrete with its high thermic conductivity exhibits many section planes of the vibration radii, and thus efficiently transfers heat. The plaster on the outside surface has a material structure of lesser density. The number of overlapping vibration radii is significantly lower, as is thermic conductivity. Of course, the U-value of the wall construction is the same in winter and in summer. Varying temperature gradients are the result of different heat flow directions and the changing sequence of the heat transmission resistances ($R = d/\lambda$) of the materials.

Wall construction with thermal insulation composite system

Here, the loadbearing reinforced concrete construction features a classic thermal insulation composite system → **13**. The insulation material is for example expanded polystyrene, coated with an external plaster. The vibration radii show that heat conduction is lowest inside the insulation layer. In spite of the high vibration energy of the reinforced concrete layer, the very porous, low density material structure of the insulation material inhibits the transmission of thermal energy to the individual molecules. This layer exhibits the largest drop in temperature. This wall construction has a low U-value and good insulation properties. The direction of the heat flow has great impact on the temperature gradient. In winter, temperatures inside the concrete are high with high inner surface temperatures. Due to this high raw density, the reinforced concrete features a significant thermal capacity. Since it is situated on the inside, it can release the stored heat into the room, for example after the heating has been switched off; resulting in a relatively constant room climate. Following the large temperature decrease in the insulation, the temperature delta between plaster and exterior air is very small, so that the vibration radii of the molecules are strongly reduced, and the plaster exhibits almost outside temperatures.

The situation is reversed in summer. Thermal energy is transported to the interior only moderately. The plaster exhibits very high temperatures, which, in the insulating layer, decrease significantly, and result in small temperature differences between the concrete and the inside air. The high temperatures in the plaster can result in great thermal stress between plaster and insulation, and can thus cause crack damage. The colour of the façade should not be too dark because the high degree of radiation absorption of dark surfaces further increases the heating of the plaster.

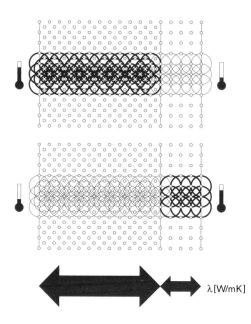

λ [W/mK]

12

Single-shell wall construction
The exterior loadbearing reinforced concrete wall is plastered on the outside.

Wall construction with interior insulation

With this external wall construction, the thermal insulation is placed on the inside → **14**. Analogously to the previously shown schematics, the intensity of heat conduction is illustrated by the arrangement of the vibration radii. In winter, the fact that the insulation layer is placed on the inside causes the temperature gradient to shift toward the inside. As a result, the temperatures inside the concrete and the external plaster are very low and approach the ambient outside temperature. Due to the low thermal capacity of the materials at the interior wall surface, rooms insulated on the inside heat and cool quickly. Analogously to the temperature gradient, the dew point of the water vapour also shifts toward the inside. This can lead to problems concerning moisture proofing. More on this can be found in Chapter 3, 'Moisture'.

In summer, the situation is reversed. The greatest temperature decrease occurs in the interior zone. On hot summer days, the exterior of the entire massive building heats up slowly but steadily due to the high thermal capacity. This storage mass is lacking on the inside. If a lot of thermal energy is introduced into a room with interior insulation, for example through large window areas, low thermal capacity of the plaster and the wall insulation can result in high inside temperatures that greatly reduce the comfort level.

Rear-ventilated wall construction

A rear-ventilated exterior wall construction consists of an insulating layer, followed by an air layer, in which air flow occurs → **15**. Generally, these layers feature strong ventilation. Within solid materials the heat is transmitted via heat conduction in the known manner, depending on the vibration radii present. In the strongly ventilated air layer, the main transmission mechanism is forced convection. In this context, the flow rate is so high that heat transmission to the air molecules occurs almost directly. In winter, the

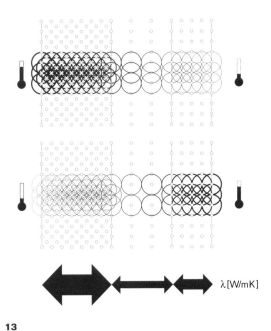

13

Wall construction with thermal insulation composite system
The insulation material is expanded polystyrene, coated with external plaster.

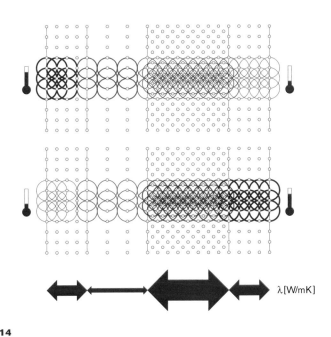

14

Wall construction with interior insulation
This exterior wall features thermal insulation on the inside. Due to the low heat storage capacity of the materials on the interior wall surface, indoor spaces insulated on the inside heat and cool quickly.

temperature in the insulation layer decreases significantly. In terms of heat transmission, the flow rate within the air layer practically separates the following layer from the rest of the layered structure. In a stationary case, the temperature in the most exterior layer almost equals the outside temperature. In the building industry, these layers are not considered part of the heat insulation. The resulting temperature decrease in the insulating material can lead to the condensation of water vapour. The air flow prevents the formation of condensation moisture and the insulation material from getting wet. Excess moisture is immediately transferred to the exterior (refer to section 'Moisture-proofing in four exterior wall types' in Chapter 3, 'Moisture').

In summer, the inside of the construction element behaves similar to a thermal insulation composite system. On the outside, the rear-ventilated façade offers advantages. The outer material layer heats up in summer. However, the air flow of the strongly ventilated air layer results in significant heat transfer, so that the temperatures in the material do not rise excessively.

THERMAL BRIDGES

Thermal bridges are zones with very different heat flows within a construction → **16**. Thermal bridges predominantly occur in areas where construction elements are joined. In contrast to undisturbed construction element areas, increased heat flows occur in these so-called disturbed areas. Principally, we differentiate between the following three types of thermal bridges:

Structural/material-related thermal bridge

These thermal bridges occur if construction elements consist of heterogenic materials. Their different building physics properties, such as thermal conductivity, raw density and specific heat capacity, for example, lead to varying heat flows. Another classic example is a reinforced concrete ceiling that penetrates a brick wall. Significantly more heat is transmitted through the surface of the reinforced concrete than through the brick material.

Geometric thermal bridge

Geometric thermal bridges occur at corners and edges of joining construction elements. In corner areas, small interior surfaces often face large, heat-transmitting exterior surfaces. In such disadvantageous situations, the heat flow condenses in the interior corner. This thermal bridge effect is particularly significant with three-dimensional construction element joints such as wall to wall to ceiling.

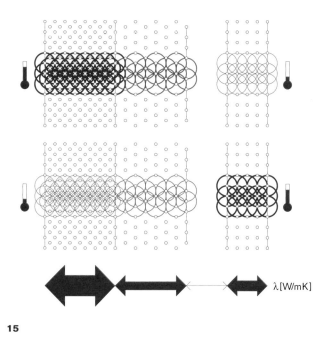

15

Rear-ventilated wall construction
The insulating layer is followed by an air layer with air flow.

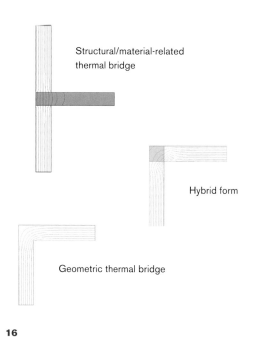

16

Different types of thermal bridges
Structural or material-related thermal bridge, geometric thermal bridge and a hybrid form of both types.

Hybrid types of structural, material-related and geometric thermal bridges

With some constructions, material-related as well as geometric thermal bridge effects can occur. One typical example are support columns in corner areas.

Usually, the increased heat transfer at thermal bridges has a negative effect on the structure of the building. One the one hand, the transmission heat loss increases across the heat-transferring building envelope, and on the other hand, thermal bridges result in low construction element surface temperatures. Water vapour can condensate on these surfaces when the dew point temperature is met, and the probability of moisture-induced building damages increases. Capillary condensation within a material is already possible at a relative humidity of 80%. Organic breeding grounds, such as ingrain wallpaper, for example, stimulate mould growth.

In order to avoid related building damages, thermal bridges must be thoroughly examined. Heat and moisture flows follow the principle of the path of least resistance. Therefore, the effects of a thermal bridge increase in the boundary areas between zones with high and zones with low insulation.

SUMMARY THERMAL ENERGY AND TYPICAL WALL CONSTRUCTIONS

In the building industry, the transmission of thermal energy is primarily described by three mechanisms: heat conduction, convection and radiation. Molecular vibration of a material and the contact between adjacent molecules result in thermal transmission via heat conduction. Convection means thermal transmission via air flow. Hereby, air molecules charged with thermal energy transfer heat to adjacent materials by flowing past them. Therefore, the heat transfer can also reverse. Radiation occurs in the form of electromagnetic waves transmitted from vibrating atoms or molecules.

The heat transition through a construction element is always linked to these three heat transfer mechanisms. Four practice-oriented wall constructions will illustrate the paths that thermal energy takes through the different material layers. The arrows symbolise the intensity of the heat conduction, in dependence of the material density. Hereby, the vibrational energy decreases continuously from high to low temperature levels.

Thermal energy acts on the wall surfaces with a convective and a radiative share. The radiative share of thermal energy largely depends on the emission ratio of the construction element surface, and the convective share on the flow rate of the air. Both phenomena lead to thermal boundary resistances, R_{si} and R_{se}, on the interior and the exterior sides. The slanted arrow visualises the reflected, radiative share.

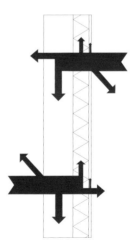

17

Schematic section through a single-shell wall construction
The exterior wall is made of reinforced concrete and a layer of plaster on the outside. The concrete layer fulfils the insulation requirement.

18

Schematic section through a wall construction with thermal insulation composite system
The exterior reinforced concrete wall features a thermal insulation composite system made of expanded polystyrene insulation and a plaster layer on the outside. Here the requirements of insulation and loadbearing capacity are met separately.

In the exterior wall made of reinforced concrete and with an exterior layer of plaster → **17**, depending on the surface quality and the emission ratio, part of the energy is reflected into the surrounding environment. The transmitted energy is transported through the material layers of the construction element via thermic conductance. The two materials feature different thermal conductivity values. Due to its lower thermic conductivity, the porous plaster transmits thermal energy less well than the concrete with its high thermic conductivity and high density.

The exterior reinforced concrete wall → **18** features a thermal insulation composite system of for example expanded polystyrene insulation and externally applied plaster. Heat conduction is lowest in the insulation layer, and highest in the concrete. In winter, the molecules in the concrete are excited to vibrate, and the heat is transmitted well to the insulation layer. The temperature gradient within the concrete layer is small, whereas it is the largest within the insulation layer. The very porous, low density material structure of the insulation material makes it difficult to transport the heat in spite of the great vibrational energy, which causes the temperature in this layer to drop the most. On hot summer days, the heat flow runs from the outside to the inside. The temperature gradient is reversed. Due to the low thermic and thermal capacity of the plaster and the insulation layers, the outside can heat up significantly, resulting in great material stress.

In principle, an interior insulation system → **19** behaves like an exterior insulation system regarding its heat transmission mechanisms; however, with reciprocal temperature gradients. Again, the low thermic conductance of the insulation layer generates the largest temperature decrease. Since the temperature gradient shifts toward the indoor space, it is mandatory to critically examine the resulting dew point when verifying moisture proofing. Due to its high mass and specific heat capacity, the concrete on the outside can store high temperatures in summer, and the exterior surfaces heat up less.

The construction shown in → **20** is a rear-ventilated wall structure with an insulation layer of mineral wool, which, again, exhibits the lowest heat conduction. The most significant difference to the other three constructions is the air layer. If heat transmission takes place in all solid materials via heat conduction, energy transfer within the air layer is also based on convection and radiation. Different thicknesses of the air layer and different air flows result in different heat transmission resistances. If the movement of the air is so strong that an air layer is strongly ventilated, the heat transmission to the air molecules in the air layer is almost complete. In this case, adjacent material layers do no longer contribute to effective heat insulation.

If condensation forms at the boundaries of the air layer, the air movement can easily transfer it toward the outside, which prevents the materials from getting wet. In summer, the interior of the rear-ventilated construction features similar properties to those of the thermal insulation composite system. On the outside, the air flow prevents that the surface of the exterior wall heats up excessively.

19

Schematic section through a wall construction with interior insulation
In principle, an interior insulation system comprises of the same heat transmission mechanisms as an exterior insulation system; however, with reciprocal temperature gradation.

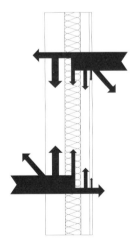

20

Schematic section through a rear-ventilated wall construction
This construction consists of a rear-ventilated wall with a mineral wool layer that features lowest thermal conductivity. The loadbearing function is taken on by the interior concrete layer.

3

Moisture

Water is the basis of human life – too little, and we would perish. Water does, however, also pose risks – in the form of torrential downpours as well as permanent moisture, especially in buildings. Every building should be planned such that it can accommodate the different aggregate states of water → **1+2**.

In this context, water vapour and its movement through construction elements is of great relevance. It is a phenomenon that is not easily explained, and one that we face in daily life. It is noticeable when the air is uncomfortably dry or muggy, when the windscreen of the car fogs up, or when condensate forms on the glass of a cool drink. The sensation is significantly more intense when we find ourselves outside in a torrential downpour without an umbrella. While body and clothing are easily dried at home, the effects on a building due to a leaking roof, window or wall are far more serious. It can quickly cause disadvantageous hygienic conditions or even structural safety problems.

In order to better understand these aspects and their effects we first examine some of the basics of the material water and its properties.

1

Upper building envelope
The upper building envelope is frequently subject to adverse weather conditions. Since apertures and joints are areas of potential leakage, they must be carefully planned and executed.

2

Leakage
Leakage caused by damage of a joint in the building envelope, resulting from temperature-related stress.

PRINCIPLES

Water, one of the main actors in building physics, has a very high heat capacity of $4.1826 \frac{kJ}{kg*K}$ (air, by comparison: $1.005 \frac{kJ}{kg*K}$) – this parameter describes the energy needed to heat it. Water serves as an excellent energy storage and carrier; common examples are heating systems and boilers in our homes as well as the hot-water bottle. Contrary to closed waterpipes or thermos flasks, water inside buildings and rooms comes in contact with air, which means that, in its fluid state, it tends to evaporate on the surfaces of construction elements.

Latent heat is necessary for this process to achieve the phase change from fluid to gaseous. Even though this thermal energy does not cause a temperature change in the dissolved water, it does withdraw energy from the vacated mass (water, wall, skin, etc.); something that we exploit when perspiring, for example, to cool our bodies → **3**. The process is based on the principle that the evaporating water molecule needs a higher potential energy to reach the greater and unordered distances in the gaseous phase. Thus, the energy is not lost, but is rather transferred to the dissolved molecule to reach entropy, i.e. to vaporise into the gaseous disorder.

The amount of evaporation strongly depends on external circumstances such as temperature, air flow rate and ambient humidity; easily observed when drying clothes. On a dry summer day, laundry dries quickly in fresh air, while it seems to take forever on a misty autumn day.

HUMIDITY

The example shows that the different aggregate states of water (solid, fluid and gaseous) lead to different physical effects and mechanisms, particularly if water is mixed with another medium: air. Air is a gas mixture of different components such as oxygen, carbon dioxide, nitrogen compounds, inert gases and water. The share of water in the air determines humidity; it can be expressed as relative humidity as a percentage or as absolute humidity (g/m^3). If the moisture content of the air increases, its density decreases because the water molecules are some of the lighter elements of the air. This influences the partial pressure ratio: with its water molecules and their movement in a defined air space, each percent or gram of moisture exerts pressure – water vapour pressure. The water vapour pressure depends on the temperature – if the

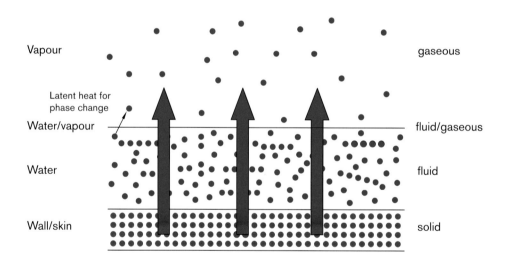

3

Evaporation

During the phase change of fluid water into vapour, the disorder of the structure increases, which requires energy. The energy is transferred to the vapourising water molecules in the form of latent heat. This process does not change the water molecules' temperature. However, the withdrawal of energy causes the skin to cool, the principle of perspiration.

air can absorb no more moisture, the so-called saturation vapour pressure is reached. If it is exceeded, water changes to a fluid state. Hereby, the partial vapour pressure can be between 0 hPa (vapourless air) and a maximum of 40 hPa (max. 4 volume percent vapour in the air). With equal relative humidity, warm air thus contains a larger absolute amount of moisture and therefore a higher partial vapour pressure than colder air. If 25°C warm air with 50% relative humidity cools by 5° Kelvin, the absolute humidity remains constant at 10 grams water per kilogram air, but the relative humidity increases to 70%.

WATER-INDUCED STRESS ON BUILDINGS

A building must be able to accommodate various types of water-induced loads without incurring damage by water, vapour and bulking (increase in volume) due to ice formation, and without creating an uncomfortable indoor climate. Thus, choices must be made in terms of which influences should be limited and in how far. Ideally, a building would be hermetically sealed against rain and pressing water → 4. This is justifiable and necessary for spaces with short durations of stay or strong exposition such as

basements. Watertight building materials are necessary such as watertight concrete or sealing material such as bitumen or PVC film. On the other hand, there are the demands of the users and construction element requirements that ask for water vapour-permeable or adaptive sealant layers to enable the exchange and transmission of moisture. This does not only mean windows, which, when opened, allow an exchange with the outside air, but also walls, for example, since they contribute to moisture regulation inside buildings. Hereby, the various possible influences on a building such as precipitation, heavy rain, building moisture and water vapour → 5 + 6 need to be carefully examined to select appropriate building elements.

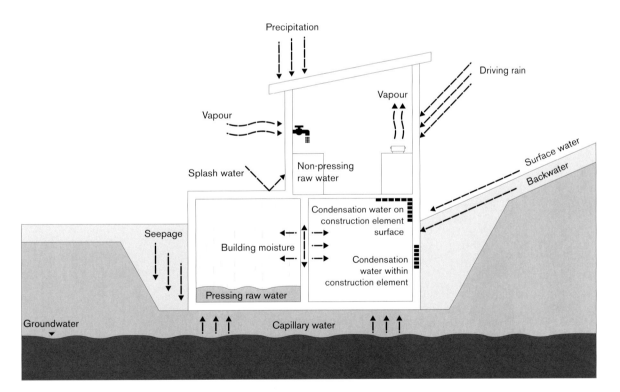

4

Building-relevant types of water
Throughout the years, a building is exposed to various types of water loads that need to be considered during planning.

The physical presence of people and/or plants as well as cooking or drying clothes raises the humidity in a space, causing several effects:

The risk of condensation water forming (i.e. settling on surfaces) increases the more, the closer the air comes to being saturated. In addition, a higher penetration pressure of the water vapour (water vapour diffusion) acts on construction elements because the increasingly saturated air (high partial pressure) pushes to the outside. Especially in winter, the air outside is dry and cold so that its partial pressure is very low. The result is that the difference in partial pressure between the inside and the outside multiplies.

The overall wall system always strives to balance the different pressure levels when the moisture conditions on the inside and the outside differ. The more porous and moisture-permeable the material, the more moisture penetrates through the wall. This can be verified with simulations, even though hand calculations according to the Glaser method (named after its developer Helmut Glaser and detailed in German standard DIN 4108) are more common. Hereby, the layers of the construction element to be examined are characterised with water vapour diffusion resistance values μ, which often feature a small, easy to diffuse inward resistance and a large, difficult to diffuse outward resistance. The μ-value determines how strong the diffusion resistance of a material is against an air layer (μ-value = 1) that crosses a water molecule. Multiplying this ratio with the layer thickness determines the water vapour diffusion equivalent air layer thickness, the s_d value, which can be added layer by layer, and thus allows for a

5

Waterproofing at grade
Waterproofing of the lower construction elements with dimpled sheets and watertight insulation against frost.

6

Detail of window joint
Window joint sealing against driving rain and water vapour diffusion.

calculational and graphic recording of the diffusional resistances of a composite construction element. For the graphic and the calculational method, the outer (−5°C, 80% relative humidity) and inner temperature and humidity conditions (20°C, 50% relative humidity) are fixed, so that a particular layer temperature can be determined by means of the heat transmission resistances R described in Chapter 2, 'Thermal Energy'. In a graph, the s_d-values are then plotted on the axis of abscissa, and the temperature-corresponding saturation vapour pressures on the axis of ordinate across the entire construction element cross-section. Hereby it is important that the smaller s_d-values are used for the path into the construction element, i.e. the low resistances, and the larger s_d-values from the expected point of condensation water occurrence onward (in an area of great temperature difference). It must be noted that according to the latest norms the graphical method requires to divide the s_d-value by the total s_d-value to normalise them to 1. However, for clarity reasons, the true equivalent air layer thicknesses are depicted → **7+8**.

7

Detail of pipe joint outside
Connection with the building below grade against pressing water.

8

Detail of pipe joint inside
Pipe penetrating through the ceiling of a fire protection section and all sealant layers.

If one tries to connect the partial vapour pressures of the true exterior conditions (1168 Pa inside and 321 Pa outside) with a line by approximating it to the exterior conditions from below, this can lead to contact points with the plotted saturation vapour pressures of the construction element layers → **9**. Since the vapour pressure in the construction element cannot rise above the saturation vapour pressure (blue progression), water condensation forms at this point or in this area – at these positions, the line of the exterior conditions comes to lie alongside the saturation vapour pressures. The progress can be visualised as a rope connecting the interior and the exterior conditions, which, sagging, is pulled tighter and tighter. The saturation vapour pressures at the different layer boundaries are fixed nails that cannot be exceeded so that the rope, when reaching such a point, would come to lie alongside the nail (see 426 Pa, 1.73 m in → **9**).

Even though this case indicates water condensation, the amount of water condensation still needs to be calculated. This value may not exceed 1 kg water per m² construction element.

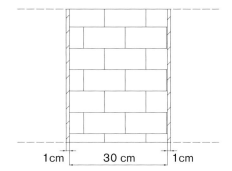

1 cm   30 cm   1 cm

9

**Graphic verification of water condensation
in a brick wall with plaster on both sides**
The graphics show the water vapour diffusion equivalent air layer thicknesses of the construction element layers, the saturation vapour pressure of the different layer temperatures (blue line) and the idealised real water vapour pressure conditions on the inside and outside (red line).

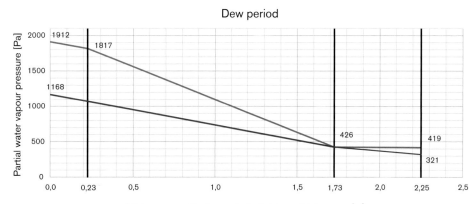

Dew period

Partial water vapour pressure [Pa]

Water vapour diffusion equivalent air layer thickness s_d [m]

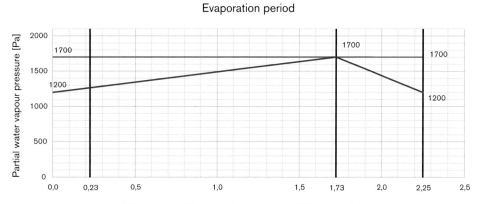

Evaporation period

Partial water vapour pressure [Pa]

Water vapour diffusion equivalent air layer thickness s_d [m]

With adjacent, capillary non-active construction elements such as fibre insulation materials, this limit can drop to 0.5 kg/m². And the amount of water must be smaller than that that can diffuse out of the construction element during an evaporation period in summer.

A permanent or even additive moisture penetration can be damaging for porous materials: not only the thermal protection but also the loadbearing capacity can suffer. Mould can form after a fairly long time, and chipping can occur in case of frost. Water condensation can occur anywhere in the construction element – anytime that the temperature of the water vapour stream drops below the dew point. Water condensation can also form on surfaces if the construction elements are not sufficiently insulated.

This effect can be used specifically to protect construction elements. It is more difficult to achieve a high degree of insulation around windows, for example; however, as the profiles are usually made of moisture-proof materials there is no risk of damage in case of water condensation on the glass panes → 10. Condensation occurs before it can damage more porous materials – in the past this was the way the air was dehumidified, and the condensation water was drained to the outside through designated channels. Today, special drainage layers in the window frame are used to lead water condensing in this area and incoming humidity to the outside.

10

Condensation water drain on a window
If water condensation cannot be avoided or if condensation is specifically used for dehumidification, construction elements must be waterproof and a drainage system must be in place. The example shows a drainage pipe with the water dripping into a stainless steel bowl for slow evaporation.

HYGIENE

If the saturation vapour pressure in a room is exceeded, water condensation typically occurs on the room-enclosing surfaces → **11**. Specifically, if the room air, enriched with water vapour (20°C, 70% relative, 10.2 g/kg absolute humidity), cools further on a surface, it thus becomes less water-absorptive. If the air cools to 10°C close to a surface, for example, a maximum of 7.75 grams of water per kilogram air can be absorbed. This means that 2.45 g/kg water condenses on the cool surfaces. In this context, thermal bridges do not only pose an energy-related problem; concentrated cold areas cause water condensation.

Water can condense on various surfaces, which leads to critical hygienic conditions. The determining factors are the quality of the surface and its degree of contamination because a water film in combination with a nutrient medium can cause mould formation → **12**. Wallpaper, glue, as well as a certain number of pollutants suffice, even though the latter enable only superficial mould, which can be easily removed if caught early. Mould spores are harmful to health and can lead to respiratory problems and allergies even with superficial mould, but all the more if the mould growth is long-lasting and deep-seated.

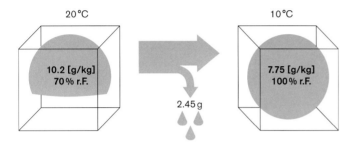

11

Water condensation
Water condensation due to cooling of 1 kg air from 20°C and 70% relative humidity to 10°C and humidity saturation.

13

Damage to building materials
Microbiological contamination and chipping caused by moisture in wooden parts.

12

Mould growth at window
Mould growth due to temperature drop in corners and roller shutter casing.

The risk of undetected mould growth is high since mould grows quickly if the inside surface of an external wall is not sufficiently heated, for example, due to air bubbles under wallpaper or unfavourable placement of cupboards, and if moisture is permanent due to a lack of air movement. Typical limits of the surface temperature and prevailing humidity are approximately 12.6 °C und 80 % relative humidity. Humidity alone suffices to stimulate mould growth; it does not require water in fluid state.

Mould growth and structural damages often occur due to leakages in otherwise well-sealed buildings because water vapour always searches for the path of least resistance. In airtight buildings, adhesive sealing joints and penetrations are frequent weak points that might fail after quite a long service life. In these areas, the flow of warm and humid air increases significantly. On its way through the construction element, the air cools down, water condenses on the inside and damages sensitive building materials through permanent moisture penetration → **18**.

14

Structural damage
Rising moisture on an interior wall with grid for humidity measurement.

15

Humidity measurement in a construction element
Destructive humidity measurement of building moisture in borehole.

16

Humidity measurement on building material
Non-destructive humidity measurement of moisture on building material.

17

Sample taking
Sample taking of the plaster to measure the moisture within the near-surface wall structure.

WATER TRANSPORT

The difference in pressure ratio is the main reason for humid air to move through a porous medium. The different conditions on the inside and the outside of a wall try continuously to reach a balance of the two partial water vapour pressures. In winter, higher indoor temperatures and accordingly more water in the indoor air cause a vapour pressure decline in the direction of the cool and, in an absolute sense, dryer exterior; the water vapour wants to penetrate the wall from the inside to the outside. Intensity and the exact path are predominantly determined by the building material and the related transportation mechanism. Hereby, the porosity of the building material and the nature of the pores play an important role.

If effusion (movement of molecules through the molecular solid of an ambient material) takes place, the pore walls are very small. Here, water molecules mostly collide with the wall rather than with each other. In turn, if the pores are larger, diffusion can take place → **19**. Hereby, the water molecules collide with each other rather than, due to the confined space, with the pore walls. The higher the gas diffusion in comparably large pore walls, the greater is the permeability of the material for water molecules. Surface diffusion along the surface of a material can occur across all pore radii. Capillary condensation describes adsorption and condensation in small pore radii, which cannot be held apart due to the fine channels. Adsorption describes the attraction of individual water molecules directly to the pore walls. Condensation, in turn, occurs when many molecule layers finally result in droplet formation. The significant factor here is the attraction between the molecules.

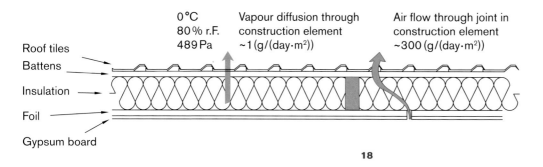

18

Water transport and vapour diffusion
The difference between planned vapour diffusion through a construction element on the one hand and air flow through a leakage on the other.

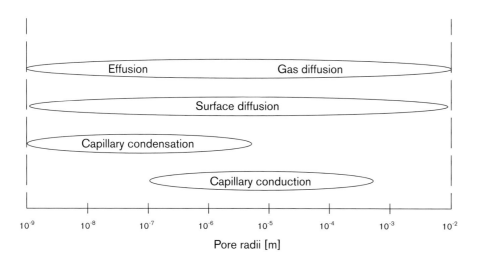

19

Pore radii
Different possible moisture movements in building materials with different pore sizes, from pure water vapour diffusion to the flow of fluid water.

Capillary conduction only occurs for a certain range of pore sizes. Within this range, fluid water can sometimes be transported against the force of gravity. The cause for this effect is the surface tension of water as well as the interfacial tension between water droplets and the material. Depending on the size of the contact angle between water droplets and the material, the greater or smaller is the attraction of the droplet to the material. With an absorbent material, for example, the water droplet lies closer to the surface than with a non-absorbent material. This describes the interfacial tension between a water droplet and the material, as does the wetting angle between the water droplet and the surface → **20**.

The smaller the pore, the higher the force of attraction on the water droplets, and the better the pore can be transported against the force of gravity. Water transmission through loose material and through joints that pose lower resistances must be examined separately. This is particularly true for natural raw and insulation materials. It is important to know how a particular building material can deal with water without incurring damage to evaluate possible damage consequences, even if the fluid water diffuses out of the wall during a period of evaporation.

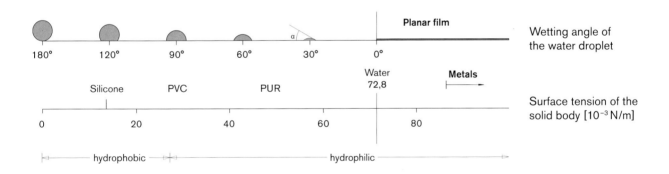

20

Wetting angle of the water droplet
Effect of different wetting angles of a water droplet on the absorptivity of different materials.

According to D. A. Rose, porous materials can accumulate moisture in six phases. In 1965, Rose published an often-cited article about transportation mechanisms in pores. In a pore, different phases of water storage can be distinguished → **21–26** To clarify the process, the pores are divided into two segments, showing the potential difference within the pore. Since, naturally, potential differences are balanced out, this is responsible for the water concentration shown.

Phase 0 represents an idealised dry material without a single water molecule present. In reality, there is always a share of molecules bound to a material.

The sporadic water molecules floating around in the pore as water vapour are absorbed by the pore wall (phase I). The area further in the centre is still dry (phase 0).

During phase II, a layer of water molecules forms on the pore wall. The degree of absorption depends on the number of diffusing molecules within the pore. Due to the potential difference between the two areas, i.e. the difference of the relative humidity in the pores, a humidity balance occurs between them. The higher the humidity at the construction element, the more diffuses into it and the greater is the number of absorbed water molecules on the pore wall. When the layer has reached a certain potential, the particles can go further inside and gradually build a layer (phase I). Because of gravitation, more molecules can be absorbed in the lower section of the wall.

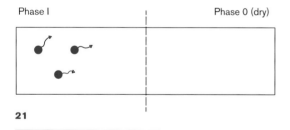

21

Phase I
Water vapour floating around in the pore is absorbed by the still dry pore wall.

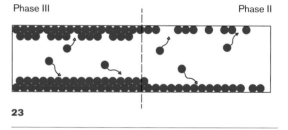

23

Phase III
Several layers of water molecules build up on the wall of the pore. First droplets begin to form.

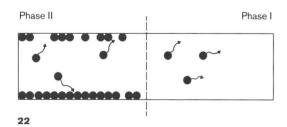

22

Phase II
Gradually, the pore wall is saturated with water vapour until a water molecule layer forms. Hereby, fewer molecules are absorbed, due to the capillary effect in opposition to gravitational forces.

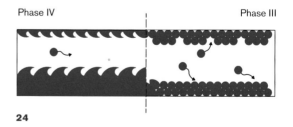

24

Phase IV
The individual droplets merge and are then transported through the pores in form of fluid water.

Several molecule layers have already formed during phase III. The resulting increased pressure leads to an almost even distribution on the pore wall. At room temperature, water molecules move freely through the air. But if they or the room temperature cool down significantly, their reciprocal force of attraction increases, and they ultimately merge into first droplets → **23** left. The potential difference within the pore is balanced further and reaches the next phase (explanation → **22**). The transportation via water vapour diffusion still predominates.

In phase IV, the droplets merge into fluid water. Due to the potential equalisation, this fluid water layer pushes further through the pore. Then, in phase V, the thickness of the absorbed layer increases further and unsaturated water transport is possible.

In phase VI, the pore is fully saturated; transportation follows Darcy's law. Henry Darcy discovered the relationship between water quantity and cross-section area of a porous medium and the resulting flow rate.

It is important to always examine material and construction in their respective entirety, i.e. to consider that other water gains might occur in addition to the water vapour transportation. All water-related influences must be taken into account, including the summation of their effects.

Pre-existing moisture-related issues must be considered as well as the location-specific conditions of the building ground. Necessary measures might include sealing against soil moisture, non-pressing water (rain water, seepage and greywater) or pressing water resulting from high groundwater. Additional drainage measures such as a porous pipe surrounding the building in case of very compact ground can lead the water away to drain off in designated areas, for example. Another stress factor for the walls can be salt, which, with its hygroscopic property, furthers the agglomeration of ambient humidity → **27**.

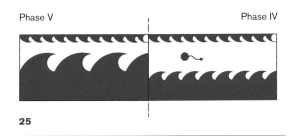

Phase V — Phase IV

25

Phase V
Unsaturated water transport is now possible within the layer of fluid water.

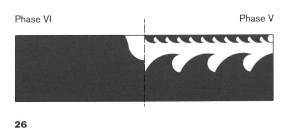

Phase VI — Phase V

26

Phase VI
The pore is fully saturated and behaves according to Darcy's law.

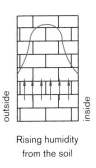

outside — inside

Rising humidity
from the soil

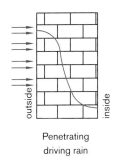

outside — inside

Penetrating
driving rain

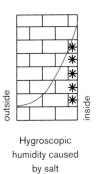

outside — inside

Hygroscopic
humidity caused
by salt

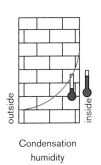

outside — inside

Condensation
humidity
below dew point

27

Moisture distribution in a construction element cross-section
Different water-related influences impact a building such as rising humidity, penetrating driving rain, humidity absorbing-materials (salt) or values below the dew point.

MOISTURE-PROOFING IN FOUR EXTERIOR WALL TYPES

Following the explanation and graphic illustration of the transportation mechanisms, these mechanisms will now be illustrated with examples. Analysing four exemplary exterior wall constructions will show the advantages and disadvantages of different moisture protection measures.

The very simplified schematic representation of moisture transportation shows the molecule level and the density in the form of scattered points. If the individual molecules or points lie far apart, the material has a low density. Molecules or points closely bundled depict higher density. The blue water molecules schematically show the transportation through a construction element. It depends on the particular construction and the material and its density whether condensation forms in the construction element.

Single-shell wall construction

A massive wall with exterior plaster → **28** can exhibit two moisture-related problems that need to be addressed. On the one hand, direct rainfall on the exterior wall; on the other hand, the influence of high humidity in the indoor space. Indoors, the molecules travel freely farther through the pores in the construction element. Since there is no insulation, the temperature within the wall construction during winter drops off toward the outside. As a result, droplets can form in the interior (when reaching saturation vapour pressure) and the construction element becomes increasingly moist, in turn resulting in increased thermic conductivity. Thermic conduction, which in a dry material only takes place via the share of solid matter, can now also take place via the filled pores.

Direct irrigation of the exterior wall causes the construction element to absorb a lot of moisture, which is then transported further into its centre. This means that over a longer time period the thermal conductivity of the exterior wall deteriorates continuously.

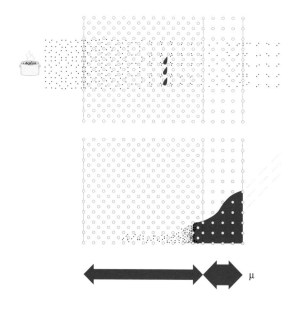

28

Single-shell wall construction with plaster
The movement of the water vapour (top) through the entire construction element is homogenous but water condensation can occur. Driving rain causes fluid water to accumulate in the plaster layer; the water can travel into the construction element by conduction and diffusion.

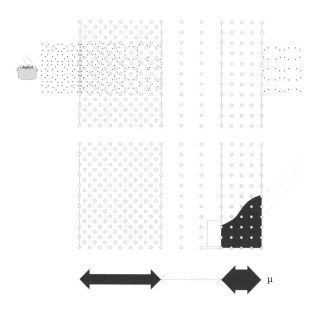

29

Wall construction with thermal insulation composite system and exterior plaster
Even though the water vapour (top) can penetrate the construction element, here, at the watertight insulation layer, it does not have good transmissivity if the joints are executed well. Thus, moisture exchange movements mainly occur within the porous materials. Driving rain causes fluid water to accumulate in the plaster layer; the water spreads in the construction element through conduction and then diffuses or evaporates on the outside.

Wall construction with thermal insulation composite system

A wall with a thermal insulation composite system behaves differently. Here, hard insulation materials with closed pores almost completely prohibit moisture transportation through the material since there are no connecting pore channels. Contrary to porous materials with high density, they also keep the construction element in the indoor space warm. This prevents increased attractive forces between the water molecules at dropping temperatures and therefore the possibility of water condensation.

Moisture transportation due to rain water also stops at the boundary layer between exterior plaster and insulation material → **29**. When the rain stops, the plaster dries without the overall moisture content of the construction element increasing.

Wall construction with interior insulation

The hard interior insulation of the exterior wall → **30** prohibits moisture transportation through this boundary layer by a large degree. The high temperature on the inside of the construction element prevents water molecules from merging so that no droplets can form.

Due to the low temperature in the outer part of the construction, a lot of moisture can accumulate in the construction element after intensive and prolonged rainfall on the exterior wall, which can only be drained to the outside if the construction is sealed on the inside. In addition, measures have to be taken that the moist indoor air cannot penetrate into the construction through leakages.

Barrier layers need to be mounted on the inside of the insulation that are sealed airtight at the joints with ceiling and floor. If such airtight film (vapour barrier) is not applied correctly, this can result in water condensation or mould.

Rear-ventilated wall construction

The rear-ventilated exterior wall construction with soft interior insulation → **31** has an entirely different impact on moisture protection. Soft insulation typically consists of fibres through which the air and water molecules can easily diffuse. Contrary to hard insulation materials, the moisture transportation is not interrupted. The enclosed or stationary air layer can also absorb water molecules, depending on the temperature. With this type of construction, water condensation usually does not occur.

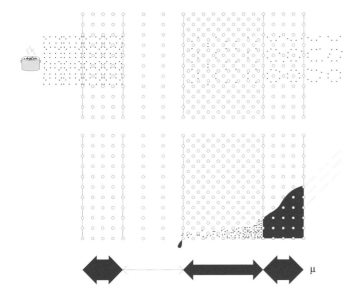

30

Wall construction with interior insulation
Even though water vapour (top) can penetrate the plaster, it does not feature good transmissivity at the insulation layer, which is watertight if the joints and connections are executed correctly. Moisture exchange movements mainly take place through the porous materials. Driving rain causes fluid water to accumulate in the plaster layer; the water spreads in the construction element through conduction and then diffuses or evaporates on the outside.

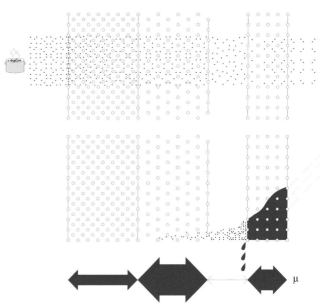

31

Rear-ventilated wall construction
Water vapour (top) can diffuse through all layers. The cooler it gets, the more probable it is for water condensation to occur on the cold outer shell. It can be drained through the air layer in the wall. Driving rain can penetrate the outer shell; however, with an air layer on the inside of the leaf, there is no further capillary conductive material. Thus, water can drop down immediately and only reach the diffusion-open insulation via evaporation.

Rainfall onto an exterior shell causes increased moisture accumulation in the plaster layer. Water that cannot be absorbed, flows down the rear-ventilated layer due to gravitational forces.

One important factor when selecting soft insulation material is its absorptive capacity. If the insulation layer becomes very wet and then dries, this can lead to shrinkage processes. The lower thickness of the layer lowers the thermal conductivity and the resistance against water vapour.

SUMMARY MOISTURE AND TYPICAL WALL CONSTRUCTIONS

In construction elements, water can be present in all of its three aggregate states, whereby pressing water, rain or condensation water represent the deciding influences. The latter develops on surfaces if the temperature falls below the dew point temperature, which leads to exceedingly high, absolute humidity and reaches saturation vapour pressure. The saturation vapour pressure represents the water vapour pressure that exists at 100% relative air humidity and a temperature-dependent maximum, absolute moisture content of the air. A regular room climate features approximately 30% to 75% relative humidity to maintain a healthy living comfort. In closed buildings, the described partial water vapour leads to water vapour flows in the construction element because indoors the vapour pressures are different from those on the outside due to the desired indoor temperature and moisture accumulation from showering, for example. Since different pressures always strive for a balance, the construction element layers undergo severe strain.

Typical constructions and concepts are derived from the many different materials available and their different handling of moisture. Basically, there are two approaches for planning a wall structure: on one hand a completely watertight concept to prevent water vapour accumulation, which, however, also prevents diffusion of water from potential building moisture or leakages out of

32

Schematic section through a single-shell wall construction
During restoration of such a non-insulated wall, the old plaster is often replaced with a rainproof plaster layer, which can lead to water accumulation.

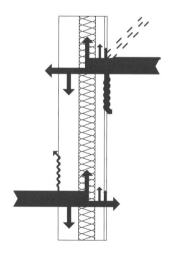

33

Schematic section through a wall construction with thermal insulation composite system
The watertight outside shell repels driving rain, but prevents outward diffusion of moisture.

the wall construction. Permeable structures, on the other hand, allow a balance between moisture accumulation in winter and the evaporation period in summer. Of course, there are combination concepts as well, the main aspect being the choice of appropriate building materials and the correct handling of events such as driving rain in order to create a functioning construction element.

Accumulation of water in fluid or gaseous state can result in damages such as salt blooming, rotting and loss of insulation effect. Expanding water during frost can lead to joint damages, cracks and chipping. It is therefore important to take all modes of action of the selected building materials into account. The extent of water vapour movement through a construction element is explained with the previously described μ-value. The schematics → **32–35** show the moisture behaviour in common wall constructions.

Single-shell wall construction

The monolithic plastered wall → **32** is a classic wall with a very diffusion-open structure; it is thoroughly wetted during driving rain. During restoration, the outside of this type of wall is often refurbished with a layer of very watertight plaster, causing potential problems. The new protective layer traps water vapour and condensate inside the building substance, and the result are visible water accumulations and damage to the plaster.

Wall construction with thermal insulation composite system

In a traditional thermal insulation composite system with watertight insulation material and exterior shell → **33**, driving rain is repelled immediately; however, moisture cannot diffuse.

Wall construction with interior insulation

The wall construction with (mostly watertight) interior insulation has the converse make-up → **34**. Most roofs are constructed in this manner, with the typical susceptibilities that need to be considered. If leakages are present, water vapour can penetrate the construction element and condensate, resulting in potential damage.

Rear-ventilated wall construction

The rear-ventilated wall construction → **35** allows for an open structure while protecting against driving rain. The air gap and the exterior shell enable diffusion. Structural details such as the anchors of the exterior shell and the connection details of the windows must be solved intelligently. One possible problem is moisture accumulation above the plinth areas (into the air layer).

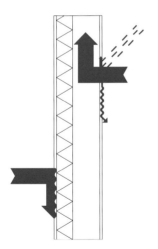

34

Schematic section through a wall construction with interior insulation
This largely diffusion-tight construction must be carefully planned to prevent damage due to water condensation in the interior.

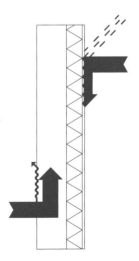

35

Schematic section through a rear-ventilated wall construction
Air gap and exterior shell enable diffusion of condensation water.

4 Air- tightness

For human beings, fresh and contaminant-free air in and around buildings is vital. In order to guarantee the necessary air change, used, warm air must be exhausted to the outside and fresh air from the outside must be fed into the building. This can happen in a controlled and purposeful manner by opening windows or installing and using ventilation systems, but also without control through leakages in the building envelope. The properties of air and the interaction between inside and outside air lead to various issues in building physics that have a direct effect on the user in terms of comfort and indoor hygienics. Hereby, the necessity of a minimum air change and how it can be accomplished in the most efficient manner plays an important role; but as important are the effects of the different ventilation strategies. The air change inside a building does not only depend on the user; the environment (air pressure) and weather conditions (wind conditions) are decisive factors too.

PRINCIPLES

Ventilation or fresh air supply has always been a fundamental need concerning indoor comfort and hygienics. Considering the modern and ever tighter building envelopes, targeted ventilation strategies are needed to maintain low indoor CO_2 levels, to limit energy losses and to regulate humidity.

The CO_2 level should be maintained at below 0.1–0.15 % of the room air volume to promote user comfort and sense of well-being. This value can increase dramatically in fully occupied rooms (conferences) or over long periods without ventilation (during sleeping), and can then put stress on the human organism. The recommendation is an air change of approximately 30 m^3/h per present user to exhaust excessive CO_2. An air volume flow of 3 m^3/h would suffice to maintain the vital oxygen volume; however, this value would not fulfil our demands on comfort, health and hygienics.

VENTILATION

Different ventilation concepts can be employed to achieve such air change rates. The principal differentiation is natural ventilation and mechanical ventilation. The first is solely based on pressure differences between the indoor space and exterior air – this is usually accomplished via traditional window ventilation. The process is driven by zonal temperature differences, for example, or by a chimney effect through warm air rising. Mechanical ventilation requires the installation of specific ventilation systems for controlled air exchange in a building. Hereby, airtightness plays an important role because defective windows, gaping joints or leakages result in uncontrolled air changes. On the other hand, extremely airtight buildings with continuous and consistently glued sealing layers (sealing foil between wall and window) can generate problematic under- or overpressure inside the building if the ventilation system is not set up correctly.

During summer, the mandated large air change rates do not pose a problem, since window ventilation, particularly at night, is the simplest manner to provide ventilation and even cooling. Ventilation effects can be optimised with dedicated constructional measures. The decisive factor is the arrangement of the ventilation openings and their size. Rooms with facing windows are beneficial as are indoor situations with a chimney effect such as lightwells or staircases. Window ventilation in rooms with windows on one side only is less efficient.

In → 1 different ventilation possibilities and their effect are compared. The choice for a particular ventilation concept ultimately depends on the cost, design aspects and various building physics requirements. Ventilation flaps, gap ventilation and ventilation openings are either based on pressure differences or are controlled with sensors, which is why the user has very little or no influence on these ventilation variants. Targeted ventilation with high air exchange rates can be achieved with simple window opening, whereby a baffle panel can be advantageous for the building construction as well as soundproofing. The air change (1/h) for the volumes related to the ventilation openings is shown in → 1. The unit specifies how much of the entire indoor air volume is changed within one hour, whereby 1/h indicates complete exchange.

In winter and with natural ventilation, indoor temperatures drop perceptibly; depending on the type of ventilation and the characteristics of the room this is accompanied by significant energy losses. With window ventilation, short ventilation bursts are energetically economical because the room volume can be exchanged through a large ventilation opening during just a few minutes. Even though the warm air escapes, more or less massive indoor construction elements do not cool off, so that the indoor air can be heated back to comfortable levels within a short period of time. However, light constructions or inside-insulated surfaces reduce this effect. A window that is only tilted open and therefore features a smaller ventilation opening prolongs the necessary time for the air to be exchanged, and the adjacent surfaces cool down. Old buildings are rarely equipped with mechanical ventilation, and

1

Ventilation openings in the façade
There are many possibilities for façade-integrated ventilation. The image shows the achievable air change, the controllability and the effects on sound protection. The air change indicates how often the entire indoor air volume is exchanged in one hour.

	Air exchange rate [1/h]	Adjustability	Acoustic protection	
Ventilation through window	0.5–20	medium	low	
Ventilation through window with exterior impact pane	0.5–5	low	high	
Ventilation flaps	1–3	low	low	
Gap ventilation	0.5–2	high	high	
Ventilation opening (sensor- or pressure-controlled)	0.5–2	low–medium	very high	

even during restoration such systems are not retrofitted because of the cost for retroactive installation. One exception are exhaust systems for interior, window-less sanitary facilities because they are hygienically indispensable. In many cases the solutions are small exhaust fans, mounted decentrally in the relevant rooms. Hereby, care must be taken that air from neighbouring rooms can flow into these spaces in order to exhaust water vapour from showering, for example.

Unused, the humid and warm air flows to the outside, thus generating additional energy loss in old buildings since opaque construction elements are usually not well-insulated anyway. Heat exchangers could be employed to reclaim the thermal energy contained in the used air.

Increased energetic and normative requirements related to user comfort demand a responsible approach to indoor ventilation → 2. Energy losses can only be minimised and indoor hygienics optimised with thoughtful ventilation concepts.

Free ventilation

Typically, manual ventilation suffices in residential living quarters – even at night. Users should enable regular air change to guarantee hygienic conditions and to protect the building. This is particularly important after window exchanges; not every user knows that previous leakages on the old window frames ensured air change, even if uncontrolled, which is no longer the case with the new, very airtight and less conductive windows. As a consequence, the non-insulated wall becomes the coldest construction element. This means that these areas are prone to water condensation, particularly when high humidity levels occur due to insufficient window ventilation. Previously, with the old windows, the condensation water accumulated on the panes of the less insulating windows.

Percentage of ventilation-related heat loss

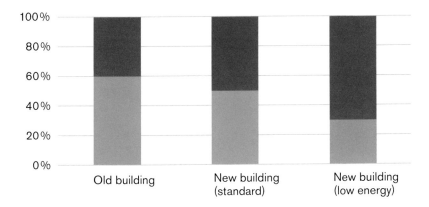

Transmission heat loss

Ventilation-related heat loss

2

Ventilation-related energy loss
Share of ventilation-related losses of the overall heat loss of buildings with different energy ratings without ventilation system.

Decentralised ventilation

With decentralised ventilation and so-called self-ventilating window frames, an integrated flap changes its position in dependence of air pressure differences between inside and outside, and thus enables air change. The user cannot influence this type of ventilation; it is only meant for room hygienics and to ensure a minimum air change. Only a few of these frame-integrated window ventilation systems allow to reclaim thermal energy through small heat exchangers; and they are significantly more expensive. The performance of these flaps is debatable since it is subject to wind direction and intensity, and the flaps can get dirty and wear out. In addition, they form an energetically weak area in the frame.

Central ventilation

Central ventilation systems are the most expensive and elaborate type of controlled building ventilation. Due to less constructional effort, central exhaust systems are a slightly less expensive alternative. However, they only 'dispose' of used air, for example through an exhaust pipe connecting bathrooms on adjacent storeys, and they require openings in the exterior shell of the building and the room-separating doors to allow for fresh (cold) air supply. This means that one central exhaust pipe is needed. The advantage in comparison to the decentralised variant is the possible re-use of the warm exhaust air with a heat pump and the larger central fan.

But if the exhaust air is to be exploited with a central heat exchanger, it is recommendable to install a supply and exhaust system. An operation without a heat exchanger is theoretically possible, but not very sensible considering the constructional effort. The configuration of the system can vary depending on the demand: an air humidifier and dehumidifier can be integrated, or the entire air-conditioning is configured as part of a heating/cooling system, so that the ventilation system incorporates an air heating system to save additional transfer surfaces. It is wise to install at least a heat exchanger because it recycles 90–95 % of the lost ventilation heat back into the building.

When planning to install a ventilation system in old or new buildings, their general life span of only 30 years should be taken into account. And the maintenance requirements as well as the hygiene of the entire system may not be underestimated. Many users or inhabitants of a building with a central ventilation system consider it uncomfortable that the constant air change in winter causes the air to be too dry. This can lead to chronic respiratory problems, which, however, could be better controlled by short-term window ventilation on dry days.

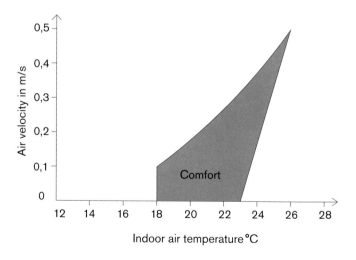

3

Sense of comfort with varying temperature and air velocity
The experimentally determined comfort tolerance in dependence of air velocity and indoor air temperature.

DRAUGHT

Next to the temperature, indoor comfort is chiefly determined by air velocity. Many people sense flow rates in excess of 0.2 m/s as uncomfortable draught. Such disadvantages usually occur with incorrectly adjusted, mechanical climate and ventilation systems, since they introduce the air in a directed manner and with pressure. Thus, if draught occurs, the exhaust openings and their orientation must be adjusted. However, uncomfortable air velocity can also occur with natural ventilation, a common sensation.

In many old buildings, leakages cause draught; especially windows are areas of concern, which is why formerly wing chairs were placed with the back toward the window to protect from the cold air flow. Strongly radiating (convective) heat sources such as fireplaces or cold air accumulation on large glass panes can also cause draught. The latter continuously cools down the rising warm room air when it passes along the pane in a way that fall velocity reaches an uncomfortable level.

The comfort diagram → **3** hows a generally valid area of comfort for a certain combination of air temperature and air velocity. Even very low air flow rates can cause discomfort, while they are tolerated more easily when temperatures are high – understandably when considering the comfortable effect a fan has on a hot summer day.

In addition, there are various turbulences in the air. Hereby, the sense of comfort is mainly influenced by the flow characteristics of the air. The comfort level is higher if the air inside a space is distributed without noticeable turbulences, whereas highly turbulent air is quickly perceived as uncomfortable. Those two factors are recorded in norm DIN EN ISO 7730, which interprets the sense of thermal comfort and establishes related criteria.

Accordingly, low and homogenous air movements provide for comfortable conditions, particularly in cold rooms in winter. Thus, short-term window ventilation and building envelopes with the highest possible degree of airtightness do not only save energy-related cost but increase the sense of comfort noticeably; even sealing door gaps with door pillows can help to prevent uncomfortable draught.

AIR PRESSURE

Another factor influencing buildings is caused by the hydrostatic air pressure that is normal and omnipresent on the earth's surface. It corresponds with the height of the air column that acts on a particular area, and is approximately 1013 hPa at sea level; equivalent to about 1 bar. The measurement unit N/m^2 (Pa) is easier conceivable; it expresses with how much force the air acts on a surface.

Because human beings are used to the prevailing air pressure of their respective areas of habitation, the air pressure inside residential living quarters is oriented on the outside air. However, temperature changes and particularly technical equipment can cause a pressure imbalance in very airtight buildings, which puts stress on the airtightness of the building. This imbalance is desired when overpressure systems are installed in hospitals, for example, to prevent germs from entering the building with the outside air.

A much more crucial factor, however, is the impact of wind pressure on the windward side of the building (overpressure), and wind suction on the downwind side (underpressure). The result is a large pressure difference with respect to the static air inside the building, which continuously strives to balance out. In such cases, leakages in the building envelope are used to let air flow into the building volume (overpressure) or to exhaust air (underpressure). Both processes subject the structure to a dynamic load → **4** that can eventually create leakages in initially airtight shells because weak bonded joints, for example, can lose adhesion → **5**.

This process can be dealt with normatively by inspecting a building with a blower door test to detect different areas of pressure. This test is described in the following section.

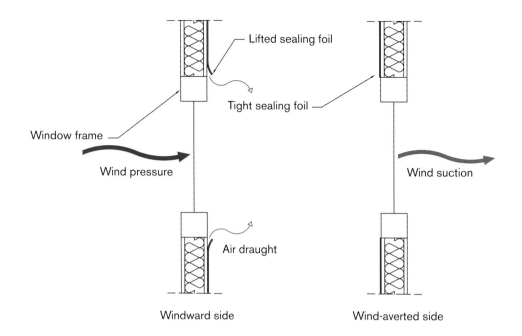

Lifted sealing foil

Tight sealing foil

Window frame

Wind pressure

Wind suction

Air draught

Windward side

Wind-averted side

4

Wind pressure and wind suction occurring around a building
Lightweight constructions are subjected to two different types of loads, which causes sealing foil on the interior to be sucked onto the construction in the low pressure area and lifted off the construction in the high pressure area; the result is cold air penetrating the building.

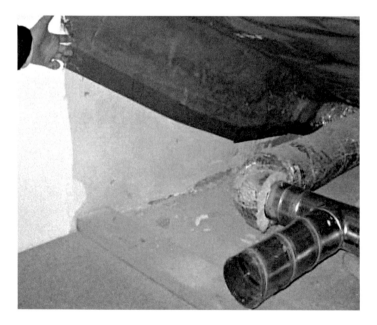

5

Defective connection of the sealing layer in the roof
The sealing foil was not glued properly in some areas, and is subjected to stress through many penetrations.

Blower door test

Airtightness of buildings can be tested with the so-called blower door test, a test that benefits the energy balance assessment. The name of the test is derived from the typical method: an open entry door, for example, is sealed as tightly as possible with a frame with an integrated fan. When all unavoidable discontinuities such as drains or ventilation openings toward the outside are sealed, this fan imposes an over- or underpressure of 5 Pa on the entire test area. In the case of lightweight constructions, it is sensible to generate both pressure differences to ensure that a sealing foil that is sucked onto the construction in case of underpressure, does not fail in case of overpressure either. To record the tightness, the flow necessary to generate and maintain the pressure difference of 50 Pa is evaluated → **6+7**.

7

Installed blower door test setup
The fan is integrated into an entry door in an airtight manner and controlled by a laptop computer so that ventilation losses can be immediately recorded and evaluated.

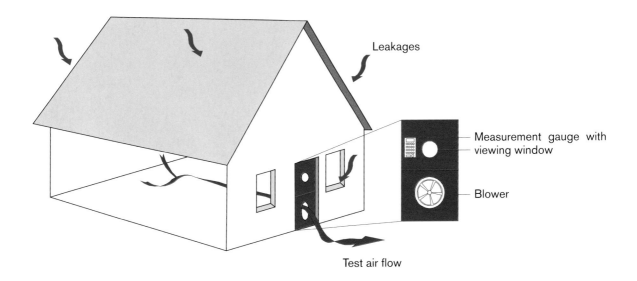

Leakages

Measurement gauge with viewing window

Blower

Test air flow

6

Blower door test setup in an underpressure configuration
The entire building is put under 50 Pa underpressure. The air flow penetrating through leakages (window, door and roof connections, joints or pipe penetrations) is measured and offset against the entire building volume to obtain the air change rate to be evaluated.

Handling apertures in the building

Necessary apertures such as around toilettes or exhaust hoods must be sealed for the tightness test so that they do not falsify the result.

Opening to exterior

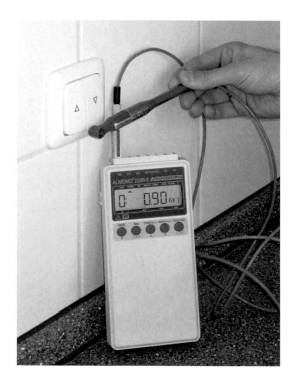

9

Leakage in window joint

The sealing was not executed correctly during window installation, which led to draught in the area of the window sill.

10

Leakages at installations

Installations and related pipes and ducts can cause measurable leakage (flow measurement).

Hereby, the building or room volume again plays a role because the result yields a ventilation number:

$$n50 = \frac{\text{Volume flow}}{\text{Building volume}} \left(\frac{1}{h}\right)$$

n50 = Air change rate at 50 Pa under-/overpressure

According to the norm, the requirements for buildings with natural window ventilation are currently n50 < 3,0 h^{-1} without mechanical conditioning and ventilation systems, and n50 < 1,5 h^{-1} with mechanical conditioning and ventilation systems. The higher requirements when employing mechanical conditioning systems can be explained with the goal to achieve a very directed air change.

Openings and penetrations are the most common causes for measured leakages; the leakages result from either faulty execution or inadequate products with low durability → 8. Other factors are damages, material embrittlement, setting or similar aspects → 9.

Discontinuities in airtightness can also occur in massive construction element surfaces; for example, when a masonry joint is washed out or air finds its way through the chambers of hollow checker bricks all the way to a wall socket → 10. Such defects are especially critical, if they cause warm humid air to condense on cooler construction elements and condensation water results in damages.

Various tools are available to detect defects: a flow measurement meter detects incoming or outflowing air flows → 13, a fog machine clearly visualises air flows and leakages → 11+12 and an infrared camera (thermography) reveals general optical defects. The camera visualises outflowing warm air and cooled areas with different colours, and thus complements a fog machine.

11

Fog machine for leakage detection indoors
A fog machine displays draught and therefore leakages.

13

Leakage detection with air flow meter
Defects at joints can be detected and quantified with an air flow meter (anemometer).

12

Fog machine for leakage detection outdoors
It is important to know exactly where air flows from the inside to the outside to fix leakages. A roller shutter casing, as shown here, is a typical area of leakage.

SUMMARY AIRTIGHTNESS AND TYPICAL WALL CONSTRUCTIONS

CO_2 emissions in breathing air and other vapours (for example, adhesives in furniture) make air change in buildings mandatory. Typically, this is accomplished with operable windows. In winter, short-term window opening is possible to prevent the concentration of harmful gases or too much humidity that stimulates mould growth.

In the case of building restoration or when windows are exchanged, previously existing window gaps and joints are eliminated, which makes it necessary to create a ventilation concept to prevent future problems. One solution are ventilation systems; they are technically complex, costly and require regular maintenance, but they can also cover other functions such as air-conditioning, ventilation and humidification/dehumidification. Unintentional ventilation results from leakages in the construction that can be caused by material embrittlement and flawed planning or execution.

In the relatively airtight thermal insulation composite system → **15**, air permeability is minimised in two layers. But there is the risk that air can penetrate at joints or lead-throughs, mainly for dowels for the insulation or installations in connected air chambers of hollow checker bricks that then cause the typical draught flowing out of wall sockets. Since joints, installations and connection details are the major cause for draught, they should be carefully considered during the planning process. Due to the nature of the construction, interior insulation bears greater risk of leakages, particularly in the corner areas, because there are large connecting areas with the adjacent construction elements and great potential for element movements that the joints must compensate → **16**. However, in terms of airtightness, this type of setup with two layers is more beneficial than a single-shell construction → **14**, since with the latter every leakage has noticeable consequences. On the other hand, this immediateness has the advantage that defects are detected quickly, whereas water accumulation in the centre of multi-layer constructions is often only detected after a longer period of time. The simple and robust construction also allows for fast repairs of joint damages.

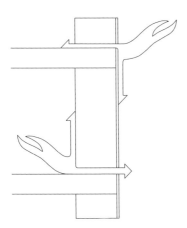

14

Schematic section through a single-shell wall construction
Since this non-insulated construction consists of one layer only, joints and leadthroughs are not covered, which increases the risk for leakages.

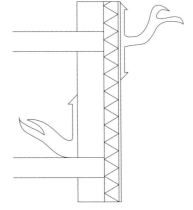

15

Schematic section through a wall construction with thermal insulation composite system
This double-layer setup minimises air permeability.

The wall with air layer and outer shell → **17** is a constructional particularity, because it behaves similar to a thermal insulation composite system if the air layer in the gap is static. It thus offers several possible airtight layers, whereby care must be taken to plan window openings thoughtfully to fulfil all requirements. The outer shell sustains direct wind loads so that they have only weak impact on the indoor air space.

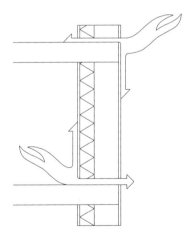

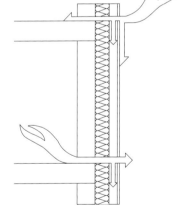

16

Schematic section through a wall construction with interior insulation
The high number of joints and lead-throughs increases the risk of leakages.

17

Schematic section through a rear-ventilated wall construction
The airtight insulation layer can cover small potential leakages in this multi-layer construction.

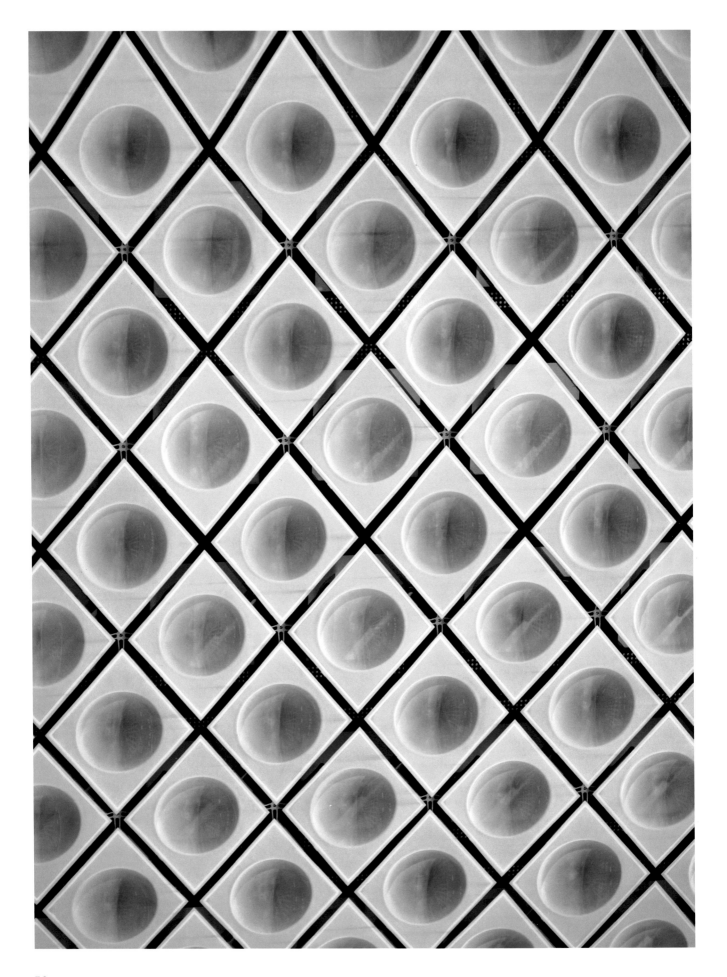

5
Acoustics

Since most of the sound sources that we encounter in our daily life cannot be switched off or avoided, and the demand for quiet living and working areas grows continuously, sound protection plays an increasingly important role in the construction of buildings. Architects or engineers should include it early in the planning process because good sound protection cannot be retrofitted at all or only at major cost and labour expenditure. The term sound protection means all measures that prevent or weaken sound transmission. Fundamental knowledge of the physics of sound propagation must be available in order to be able to develop a well-functioning sound protection concept. For this reason, the following section aims to advance into the topic 'Acoustics' with comprehensible terminology. The basic knowledge about acoustics thus attained is then used to explain the basic influences impacting the sound-insulating of wall and ceiling constructions against airborne and impact sound. Four typical wall constructions are used as examples to illustrate these effects. Since next to sound protection within a building and against exterior sound, the sound quality inside a room also has a significant effect on our sense of comfort, the last section on 'Room acoustics' examines these types of influences.

PRINCIPLES

Mammals, including human beings, sense sound via sound waves. But what are sound waves? 'Sound' describes a mechanically generated, sinuous vibration – the sound source. It spreads circularly in gases (airborne sound), fluids (liquid-borne sound) and solids (solid-borne sound), and, from a certain intensity onward, is within the hearing range of the human ear. Since all of these media consist of molecules that move constantly but at varying degrees (Brownian movement), they are stimulated in different manners, and thus transfer sound. In gases and fluids, sound energy can only propagate in the longitudinal direction, i.e. parallel to the direction of propagation of the sound wave (longitudinal wave), because the molecules inside these media are not connected to one another. In solids, on the other hand, the molecules are elastically connected, allowing for the sound energy to propagate in many different ways. The most important type of propagation in building physics is the bending wave. Hereby, the molecules move in cross-direction, i.e. perpendicular to the direction of propagation (transverse wave), as well as in the longitudinal direction of the sound wave, resulting in an angular movement of the molecules → **1**.

1

Types of sound waves
Above left: longitudinal wave – sound only propagates in the longitudinal direction, above right: transverse wave – sound only propagates in the cross-direction, below: bending wave – sound propagates simultaneously in cross- and longitudinal direction, leading to an angular movement of the molecules.

The general principle of sound propagation in air → **2** is that the sound wave propagates as the energy of the sound pushes the molecules together and apart in an oscillating movement. The result are areas of higher air pressure and areas of lower pressure (based on the naturally prevailing atmospheric air pressure of approx. 101,300 N/m²). The more these areas differ from the atmospheric pressure, the higher or lower is the so-called sound pressure p [N/m²] = [Pa] (p is also called amplitude, i.e. the maximum deflection of a sound wave). The speed with which these pressure changes occur is called sound particle velocity v [m/s], the propagation speed of the sound wave itself is called sound velocity c [m/s]. Hereby, the sound velocity in air is the lowest (approx. 340 m/s), higher in water (approx. 1500 m/s) and the highest in solids (steel 5000 m/s).

The sound wave → **2** shows a sinuous path, corresponding to the definition of a tonal sound (harmonic vibration). A tonal sound consists of a single frequency, the unit is Hertz (Hz). Hereby, the frequency specifies with how many vibrations per second a sound wave propagates. A vibration describes the cycle 'atmospheric pressure – overpressure – atmospheric pressure – underpressure – atmospheric pressure'. Mathematically, frequency is therefore expressed as the reciprocal value of a periodic time in seconds.

$$f = \frac{1}{T} \left[\frac{1}{s} \right]$$

with   f   Frequency in Hz
       T   Periodic time in s

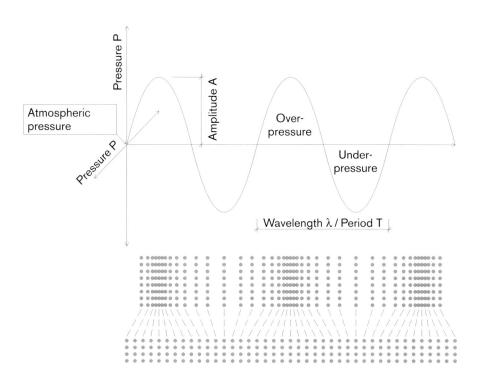

2

Principle of airborne sound propagation
Sound waves propagate as the energy of the sound pushes the air molecules together and apart in an oscillating motion. The consequence is underpressure and overpressure related to the atmospheric pressure. The oscillating motion of overpressure to underpressure is defined as vibration. The frequency describes the number of vibrations per second.

If a sound wave propagates with a high number of vibrations per second, meaning if it has a high frequency, the human ear perceives it as a high, 'light' tonal sound. If the frequency is low, the tonal sound is perceived as low and 'dark'. Hereby, human hearing depends on the age of the person, the genetic predisposition and permanent environmental influences (street noise, discotheque, etc.). Different frequency ranges according to different tasks can occur during planning → 3. These ranges are oriented on human hearing as well as on what is technically sensible and feasible.

An overlay of different sounds whose frequencies are related to each other by simple whole number ratios, generate a tonal sound. A noise occurs when the overlaying frequencies are not related to each other by simple whole number ratios, i.e. the frequency ratios are chaotic → 4.

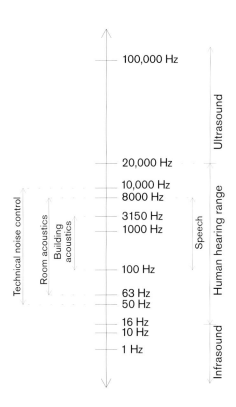

3

Illustration of the acoustic frequency ranges specified for planning
The frequency ranges specified for planning are oriented on human hearing and on what is technically sensible and feasible. But in certain cases, it can make sense to examine the frequencies below and above these ranges.

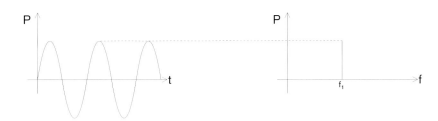

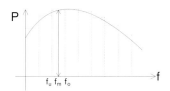

4

Sound pressure p plotted over time t
From above left to below right: pure sound with related frequency; a complex tone consisting of three sounds and therefore three frequencies that are related by simple whole number ratios; a sound consisting of overlaying sounds with a chaotic frequency ratio, shown here with its frequency band, separated in frequency ranges with the cut-off frequencies f_o, f_u and the according centre frequency f_m.

The last parameter of a sound wave to be mentioned is its wavelength λ or its period T. As already mentioned → **2**, both terms describe the distance of two successive phases. Wavelength indicates a position change of the sound wave and period denotes a chronological change. The following relationship exists between frequency, wavelength and sound velocity:

$$f = c / \lambda$$

with f   Frequency [Hz]
      c   Sound velocity [m/s]
      λ Wavelength [m]

Since sound propagation originating from a sound source does not only take place in one direction but rather in a three-dimensional space, it is called a sound field. This field can be described with two energy parameters:

Sound power P [W] = [J/s]
Sound power describes the sound energy that is emitted from a sound source as airborne sound over a specific period of time. Sound power only depends on the sound source.

Sound intensity I [W/m²]
Sound intensity is defined as sound energy that is transported vertically through an area of $1\,m^2$ over the period of 1 second. Since sound intensity is therefore a vector quantity, it can be used to localise the direction of a sound wave and the related sound source.

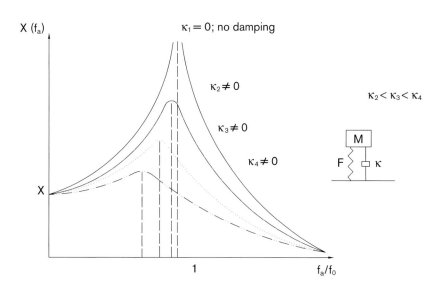

X (f_a) = Amplitude of the induced frequency
f_a = Stimulation frequency
f_0 = Natural frequency
X = Resonant frequency
κ = Damping (friction)

5

Relation between natural and resonant frequency
Natural frequency and resonant frequency can only be equated if the stimulated system does not have any damping properties, which does not exist in nature. Therefore, in physical terms it is not correct to equate the two terms.

Sound propagation in a room depends mostly on the resilience, the mass and the damping (friction) of the material to be crossed. In a double-shell construction element, an insulation or air layer, for example, acts as a spring between the two shells (masses). The shells and the spring act as an additional damper (through friction) for the sound energy. Still considering a double-shell construction element, its masses including the resilience (mass-spring-mass system) and damping create a natural frequency f_o. This is the frequency at which the system oscillates, if, after an initial sound impact no further stimuli or frictional forces are present. If sound energy strikes a construction element with a frequency similar to the natural frequency, resonance occurs, i.e. the natural oscillation of the system is enforced by the sound impact. The closer the two frequencies (natural frequency and excitation frequency), the stronger the resonance.

If the oscillation amplitude of the system reaches its maximum through the impacting sound energy, this is called resonant frequency. If there is no spring in a system, such as is the case with a single-shell construction element, the vibration can build up until a resonance catastrophe occurs, i.e. the system is destroyed. Often, natural frequency is equated with resonant frequency. This would be the case in an ideal system without damping. However, such systems do not exist in nature. Therefore, in physical terms, it is not correct to equate natural frequency with resonant frequency, if the sound amplitude is taken as a basis → **5**.

To evaluate what human beings perceive as 'noise', building physics refers to the sound pressure created by the sound power of a sound source. This measured value depends on the distance from the sound source and on the acoustic properties of the environment. Everything seems louder in an empty space with bare concrete walls than in an entirely furnished room. The sound intensity level L is used to describe sound pressure mathematically. It specifies the ratio between the amplitude of a sound event and the so-called base sound pressure (p_0). Hereby, p_0 corresponds to the tested human auditory threshold ($2 \cdot 10^{-5}$ Pa). Since the human hearing range with a threshold of pain at approximately 20 Pa is very large, sound pressure is specified as a logarithmic value, i.e. as a level measured with the unit decibel (dB).

Sound intensity level

$$L_p = 10 \log \frac{p^2}{p_0^2} = 20 \log \frac{p}{p_0} \ [dB]$$

with p Instantaneous sound pressure
 p_0 Sound pressure at auditory threshold ($2 \cdot 10^{-5}$ Pa)

The logarithmic scale yields a sound level range between 0 dB (auditory threshold) and 120 dB (threshold of pain), whereby the human ear perceives level changes of approximately 1 dB. If the total sound intensity level is to be determined from various unequally loud sound intensity levels, the particular sound intensity level of the individual sound waves is determined with the following correlation:

Total sound intensity level

$$L_{p,tot} = 10 \log \sum_{j=1}^{n} 10^{0,1 \cdot L_{p,j}} \ [dB]$$

with $L_{p,j}$ Sound intensity level of the individual sounds in dB
 n Number of sound sources

In the case of several identical sound sources, this correlation is replaced by the following equation:

Total sound intensity level

$$L_{p,tot} = L_1 + 10 \cdot \log n = L_1 + \Delta L_1 \ [dB]$$

with L_1 Sound intensity level of the individual sounds in dB
 n Number of identical sound sources
 ΔL_1 Increase of sound intensity level at n identical sound levels

The so-called weighted sound intensity level addresses the fact that human beings perceive sound intensity levels differently depending on frequency and subjective sensation (e.g. low sounds are perceived quieter than high sounds). Modern measuring devices automatically lay a filter over the recorded sound level and thus adjust the result to the loudness perception in dependence of the frequency. Hereby, a correction value is used as the basis by means of so-called reference curves. The most generally established curve is the A-reference curve; a weighted sound intensity level is thus identified by L_A, the unit is called dB(A).

BUILDING ACOUSTICS

Building acoustics (structural sound protection) deals with sound protection within buildings and against exterior noise, aiming at protecting occupants from unacceptable sound impact. We differentiate between airborne sound protection and impact sound protection to describe the sound protection effectiveness of construction elements. Impact sound results from walking on a ceiling, for example. Hereby, sound energy is generated through the vibration of the construction element, and is transferred into the ceiling as solid-borne sound. Sound is also propagated to the air and, thus, transferred to the human ear in the form of airborne sound.

Each construction element in a building must exhibit an adequate degree of sound protection, i.e. the capability to dampen sound. The better the sound-insulating, the less the occupant is subjected to noise. Hereby, the following factors play a significant role: raw density of the material used, the possibility of transferring sound to adjacent construction elements and the construction method of the construction elements → **6**.

The following deduction can be made: the higher the raw density of a construction element or the respective material, the better its airborne sound protection capacity. (However, this statement is based on extremely simplified assumptions. Next to raw density, a material's molecular structure also plays a significant role in sound dissipation.) When multiplying the raw density with the layer thickness of the material used, the result is the so-called area-related mass, as illustrated by the following formula:

$$\text{Density thickness} \quad m' = \sum \rho \cdot d \left[\frac{kg}{m^2} \right]$$

with ρ Raw density of the material [kg/m³]
      d Material thickness [m]

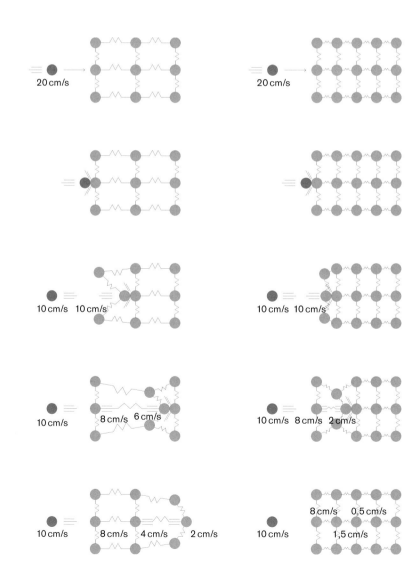

6

Solid-borne sound propagation depending on raw density
A material with low raw density transfers sound energy better because the distances between the individual molecules of the material are relatively large. In contrast, materials with a high raw density absorb sound energy faster because the molecules lie closer together.

The following simplified maxim can be derived: The heavier a construction element, i.e. the larger its area-related mass, the higher its airborne sound protection value; but also, the higher is its thermal conductivity and therefore the lower are its heat insulation properties and vice versa.

The influence of acoustical bridges must be mentioned in this context because construction elements or their shells are always rigidly connected to the loadbearing structure or to other construction elements through edge fixation. Flanking construction elements serve as the transmission path for the sound → **7**.

These transmission paths can be interrupted by completely decoupling the construction elements, for example by installing floating screed. If all connections are executed appropriately, impact sound protection between screed and concrete floor separates structure-borne sound from the other construction elements (walls, ceilings) and thus prevents its propagation. Since even the smallest acoustical bridges drastically reduce the sound protection effect and allow for sound transmission, planning and execution must be done very carefully. A classic example of such an unintended acoustical bridge occurs when, during wall plastering, small lumps of mortar get into the corner joint between floating screed and wall. A hairline crack in the plaster also suffices to locally reduce the sound protection of the wall. And the construction method plays an important role – which will be detailed in the following sections 'Protection against airborne noise' and 'Impact sound protection of ceilings'.

horizontal

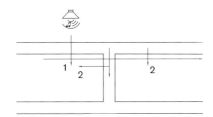

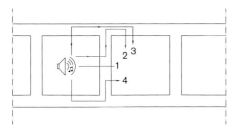

vertical

1 Directly through the separating surface
2 From the separating surface onto the flanking wall
3 Along the flanking wall or ceiling
4 Along the flanking wall across the separating surface

7

Sound transmission along other construction elements
In dependence of the position of origin, sound is transmitted along different paths via flanking construction elements.
Left: sound transmission caused by exterior noise; centre and right: sound transmission caused by interior noise.

AIRBORNE NOISE PROTECTION OF WALLS

For the protection against airborne noise, the so-called airborne sound-insulating index determines in how far a construction element can protect the occupant from sound impact. Hereby, the higher the airborne sound-insulation index of the construction element, the higher its sound insulating effect. This relates to the fact that the sound pressure level difference between transmitting and receiving space is used to evaluate the construction element.

In simple terms, the airborne sound-insulating effect of a construction element depends on its area-related mass, the sound transmission along other elements and the construction method of the construction element.

Construction methods are different for single-shell and multi-shell construction elements. A shell either consist of a single material (e.g. concrete, masonry, glass) or of several, permanently fixed layers (e.g. plastered masonry). The different layers must feature very similar soundproofing properties in order for the leaf to vibrate as a whole.

Single-shell walls

As described earlier, the sound-insulating properties of a construction element largely depend on its mass. This fundamental fact was mathematically formulated by R. Berger as early as in 1910 with the so-called Berger's mass law. It states that with each doubling of the mass or the frequency, the sound-insulating index improves by 6 dB per octave. However, the original mass law only applies to sound striking a wall perpendicularly as well as for flexible panels. (In this context, flexible does not mean that the panels can be bent. The term depends on the cut-off frequency of coincidence of the panel, which will be further explained later in this chapter.) If Berger's mass law is related to the incidence angle of the sound, the following formula and according progress of the sound-insulating index in dependence of the frequency can be derived → **8**.

Berger's mass law

$$R = 10 \cdot \log \left[1 + \left(\frac{\pi \cdot f \cdot m'}{\rho_L \cdot c_L} \cdot \cos \vartheta \right)^2 \right]$$

with R   Sound-insulating index [dB]
      m' Area-related mass [kg/m²]
      ρ Raw density [kg/m³]
      c_L Sound velocity air ($c_L = 340$ m/s)
      f   Frequency [Hz]
      ρ Raw density air ($\rho_L = 1{,}25$ kg/m³)
      ϑ Incidence angle sound

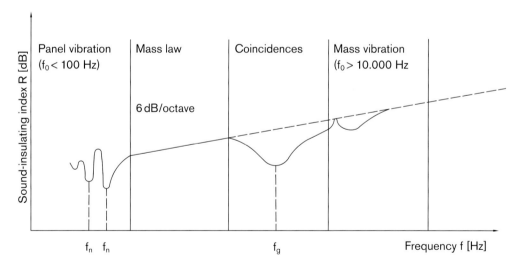

8

Progress of the sound-insulating indices in a single-shell wall
The sound incidence angle has a decisive effect on a wall's sound-insulating index. Thus, the original mass law only applies to a limited frequency range and to perpendicular sound impact. Below and above this range, at certain frequencies resonances with the natural vibration of the wall cause a reduction of the sound-insulating effect.

If the frequency of the impacting sound wave lies within the range of the natural frequency of the panel, resonances occur. This is noticeable by a reduction in sound-insulating because, in this case, the panel as a whole vibrates, and the sound energy transmits through it without significant impairment. This context is illustrated with the following formula:

Natural frequency n of a single-shell panel

$$f_n = \frac{\pi}{2} \cdot \sqrt{\frac{B'}{m'}} \cdot \left[\left(\frac{n_x}{a}\right)^2 + \left(\frac{n_y}{b}\right)^2 \right] \text{ [Hz]}$$

with f_n Natural frequency n of the panel [Hz]
        B' Flexural rigidity of the panel related
               to its width [MNm]
        m' Area-related mass [kg/m²]
        a   Dimension a of the panel [m]
        n_x Natural whole number to the xth order
        b   Dimension b of the panel [m]
        n_y Natural whole number to the yth order

The range of the panel vibration usually lies below the range relevant to building acoustics ($f_0 < 100$ Hz), but a reduced sound-insulating effect under 100 Hz can be perceived as disturbing. Above the range of the panel vibration, Berger's mathematical optimisation accords with the true values. If the sound does not strike the wall surface perpendicularly ($\vartheta \neq 0°$; angle between surface normal and sound source), the sound-insulating can be worse than Berger's mathematical values. This occurs if the bending wave in the panel, created by an airborne soundwave striking at a slant angle, has nearly the same wavelength and propagation speed as the other striking airborne sound waves. This leads to a sort of 'spatial resonance', i.e. the maximum pressure values of the airborne sound waves coincide with the maximum pressure values of the bending waves. This frequency range is called frequency of coincidence or track adjustment range → **9**.

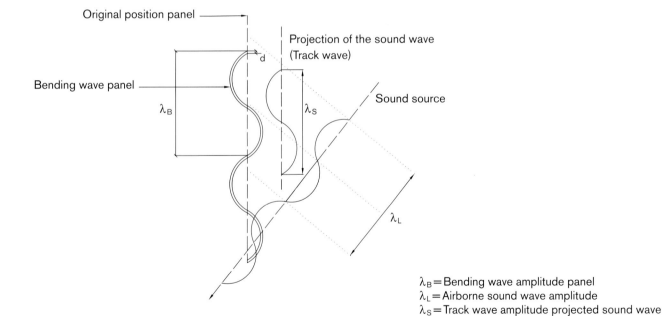

9

Principle of the coincidence or track adjustment range effect
If an airborne sound wave strikes a single-shell panel at a slant angle, it creates a bending wave inside the panel. If the bending wave has approximately the same wavelength and propagation speed, i.e. the same frequency as the following striking airborne sound waves, a resonance occurs which causes reduced sound-insulating. This frequency range is called coincidence or track adjustment range.

The lowest possible frequency at which coincidence can occur is called cut-off frequency coincidence f_g ($\vartheta = 90°$, incidence at a right angle). It can be described with the following two formulae:

Cut-off frequency of coincidence of a panel

$$f_g = \frac{c_L^2}{2 \cdot \pi} \cdot \sqrt{\frac{m'}{B'}} \ [Hz]$$

with f_g Cut-off frequency of coincidence
             or track adjustment frequency [Hz]
       c_L Sound velocity in air ($c_L = 340\,m/s$)
       m' Area-related mass [kg/m²]
       B' Flexural rigidity of the panel related
             to its width [MNm]

Flexural rigidity of a panel

$$B' = \frac{E_{Dyn} \cdot d^3}{12 \cdot (1 - \mu^2)} \ [MNm]$$

with B' Flexural rigidity of the panel related
             to its width [MNm]
       c_L Sound velocity in air ($c_L = 340\,m/s$)
       d Panel thickness [m]
       E_{Dyn} Dynamic elasticity modulus [N/m²]
       μ Poisson's ratio (typical materials $\mu = 0,35$)

Therefore, the frequency of construction elements should be outside of the building's acoustically relevant range. They are differentiated in sufficiently flexible ($f_g > 2000$ Hz) and sufficiently flexurally rigid ($f_g < 200$ Hz) (see Schild, Casselmann, Dahmen and Pohlenz, 1977, p. 133). Above the coincidence range, an improvement compared to Berger re-occurs, until the thickness mode of vibration (= vibrations between the two surfaces of a panel; can occur due to impact sound) of the panel at more than 10,000 Hz can worsen the sound-insulating again.

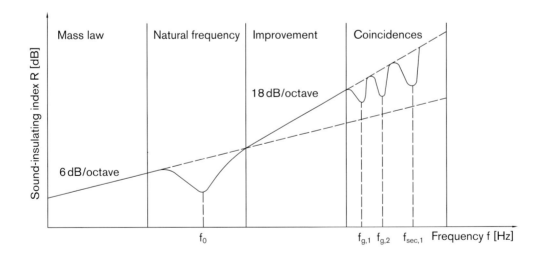

10

Path of the sound-insulating index of a double-shell construction element
Above the natural frequency, the sound-insulating index of a double-shell construction element lies noticeably above Berger's theoretically determined sound-insulating index.

Double-shell walls

Contrary to single-shell walls, the sound-insulating of double-shell walls does not only depend on the mass of the individual shells but also on the resilience of the insulation layer. This insulation layer can consist of a heat-insulating material and/or an air layer. Since the insulation layer creates a resilient connection between the shells, the path of the sound-insulating index is different than that of a single-shell wall, and there is a distinct deviation from the theoretical behaviour according to Berger → 10. This diagram highlights the following relationships:

$f \ll f_0$ If the excitation frequency is far away from the natural frequency of the construction element, a double-shell construction element features the same sound-insulating as a single-shell construction element of the same weight.

$f \approx f_0$ If the excitation frequency approaches the natural frequency, resonance occurs. The entire construction element now vibrates as if it were a single-shell construction, i.e. in phase, resulting in a significant reduction of the soundproofing properties because the sound energy transmission is very high.

$f > f_0$ Within this range, the sound-insulating of a double-shell construction element improves continuously (by up to 18 dB/octave), because the first shell does not vibrate in phase with the second. Consequently, the resilience property of the insulation layer becomes ever more noticeable.

$f \gg f_0$ If the excitation frequency reaches the cut-off frequency of coincidence of the individual shells, the sound-insulating in these frequency ranges worsens to a certain degree, but it remains better than the mathematical improvement according to Berger. In cavity layers without filling material (air layer), standing waves (cavity resonances) occur, i.e. an overlap of two counter-directional waves of the same wavelength and amplitude due to the reflection of the sound wave. They also cause dips in this frequency range. Such waves can be prevented by filling the cavities with loose mineral fibre (cavity insulation), for example.

The natural frequency of the typical double-shell systems common in the building industry largely depends on the dynamic rigidity (spring rigidity) of the insulation layer. This, in turn, depends on the dynamic elasticity modulus and the thickness of the insulation layer. A high dynamic elasticity modulus and/or low shell thicknesses are disadvantageous. Generally speaking: the lower the dynamic rigidity (i.e. the 'softer' the spring), the better are the sound-insulating properties of the insulation used. This relationship can be described with the following formula:

Natural frequency of a double-shell wall

$$f_0 = \frac{1000}{2 \cdot \pi} \cdot \sqrt{s' \cdot \left(\frac{1}{m_1'} + \frac{1}{m_2'} \right)} \ [Hz]$$

with f_0 Natural frequency [Hz]

  s' Dynamic rigidity [MN/m^3]

  m_1' Area-related mass of the first shell [kg/m^2]

  m_2' Area-related mass of the second shell [kg/m^2]

NOISE PROTECTION IN FOUR EXTERIOR WALL TYPES

The effect of raw density on the sound-insulating of a material shall be illustrated by the following examination of four typical exterior wall construction types on a molecular level. The following materials and raw densities are assumed:

Reinforced concrete $\rho \approx 2400\,kg/m^3$
Heat insulation (EPS) $\rho \approx 25\,kg/m^3$, Edyn $\approx 2.4\,MN/m^2$
Heat insulation (mineral wool) $\rho \approx 100\,kg/m^3$, Edyn $\approx 0.2\,MN/m^2$
Plaster $\rho \approx 1400\,kg/m^3$
Air $\rho \approx 1.2\,kg/m^3$ (0 m above MSL)

The figures show in a very simplified manner the sound propagation caused by airborne sound on a molecular level in a construction element. The schematics → **11–14** illustrate that the sound absorption capacity of the individual construction element layers depends on the particular raw density of the material used.

Usually this means: the higher the raw density and the thicker the construction element layer (area-related mass), the better the material or the construction element layer dissipates the airborne sound. Dissipation means that the sound energy is transformed into heat by damping (friction). However, this statement cannot simply be transferred to insulation materials because, here, the molecular structure and the dynamic elasticity modulus play an important role. This is particularly obvious in case of the rear-ventilated exterior wall construction → **14**. Even though the installed mineral wool has a relatively low raw density, the sound is strongly dissipated through the special molecule structure (fibres) and the accordingly low dynamic elasticity modulus.

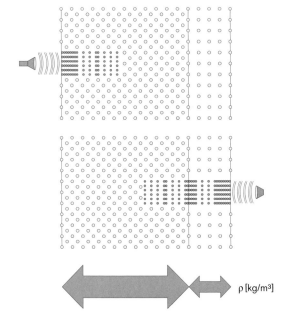

11

Single-shell wall construction
The insulation properties of a single-shell exterior wall construction approximately correspond with the theoretical sound-insulating path according to Berger.

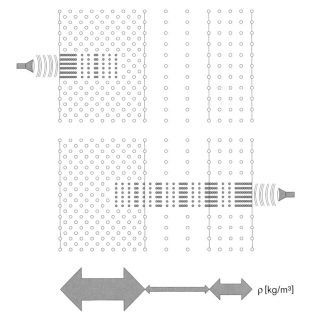

12

Wall construction with thermal insulation composite system
From a building physics point of view, the exterior wall with a thermal insulation composite system is a double-shell construction (the plaster layer of the heat insulation counts as construction element shell). Therefore, the sound-insulating index is above the natural frequency of the construction elements and clearly above Berger's theoretical sound insulation path.

IMPACT NOISE PROTECTION OF CEILINGS

For impact sound protection, the so-called assessed impact sound pressure level is used to evaluate in how far a construction element can protect the human being from sound impact. Hereby, the smaller the assessed impact sound pressure level of the construction element, the better its sound-insulating effect. This stands in contrast to the protection against airborne sound (the higher the assessed airborne sound pressure level, the higher the sound-insulating effect), and results from the fact that the sound pressure level coming into a space is measured to evaluate the impact sound protection of a construction element. Hereby, the impact sound protection of a built-in ceiling depends on the area-related mass of the massive ceiling without cover, a potentially integrated flexible suspended ceiling and the ceiling cover (floating screed or timber support) → **15**. The floor covering (carpet, parquet flooring, etc.) is not considered since it can be exchanged anytime. The positioning of the sending and receiving spaces in relation to each other also plays a role because, analogously to protection against airborne sound, sound is dissipated along flanking construction elements.

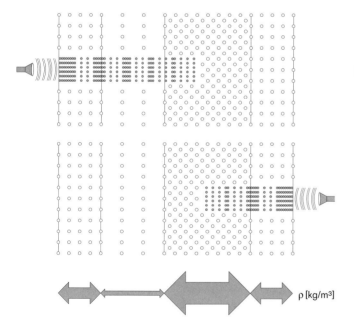

13

Wall construction with interior insulation
From a building physics point of view, an exterior wall construction with interior insulation also constitutes a double-shell construction, like the exterior wall with thermal insulation composite system above.

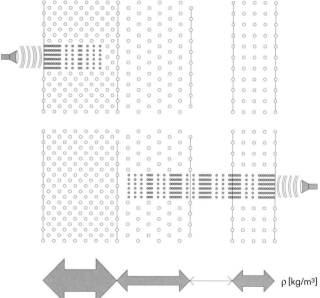

14

Rear-ventilated wall construction
In terms of building physics, a rear-ventilated exterior wall construction is a double-shell construction. Therefore, the sound-insulating index lies above the natural frequency of the construction elements and clearly above Berger's theoretical sound-insulating path.

ROOM ACOUSTICS

Contrary to architectural acoustics, room acoustics does not deal with noise protection between rooms, but rather with noise inside a room. Aspects of room acoustics are, depending on the use and requirements of the room, acoustic quality (audibility) or sound quality as well as the restriction of sound pressure levels. In a concert hall, the sound quality is of major importance. In an auditorium, optimum listening conditions are critical, and in a workshop with loud machinery the focus lies on reducing the sound pressure level. These different requirements (sound quality, ensuring audibility, reducing sound impact) can be controlled with the sound-insulation properties of the surfaces inside the room. Methods are targeted reflection and absorption/dissipation of sound energy. The ratio of reflection and absorption describes the sound-absorbing properties of a material. It is specified with the frequency-dependent sound absorption coefficient, as illustrated in the following formula:

Sound absorption coefficient of a material

$$\alpha = \frac{I_{abs} + I_{trans}}{I_{tot}}$$

with α Sound absorption coefficient [-]
I_{abs} Absorbed sound intensity [W/m^2]
I_{trans} Transmitted sound intensity [W/m^2]
I_{tot} Total incident sound intensity [W/m^2]

If α equals 0, the sound energy is completely reflected by the material in question (hard-walled, e.g. concrete); if α equals 1, the entire sound energy is absorbed (soft-walled, e.g. mineral fibre). Multiplying the absorption coefficient with the surface of a material that faces the room results in a so-called equivalent sound absorption area A, which can be described as follows:

Equivalent sound absorption area

$$A = \alpha \cdot S \ [m^2]$$

with A Equivalent sound absorption area [m^2]
α Sound absorption coefficient [-]
S Surface in question, facing the room [m^2]

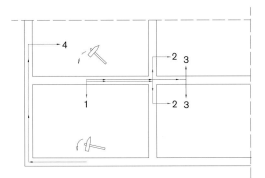

1 Directly through the separating surface (perpendicular)
2 From the separating surface onto the flanking walls (diagonal)
3 Along the separating surface (horizontal)
4 Along the flanking wall across the separating surface (bottom to top)

15

Transmission paths of solid-borne sound caused by impact excitation
The construction element excited by solid-borne sound can dissipate sound energy via four possible paths.

The equivalent sound absorption area determines how many square metres of the material in question completely absorb the incident sound. Since, in addition to walls, the floor and the ceiling, there are also furnishings (A_{fur}) and people (A_{pers}) in a room, the total equivalent absorption area A_{tot} of a room consists of the sum of all equivalent sound absorption areas plus the equivalent sound absorption areas of the furnishings (furniture, etc.) and the people present in the room. The relationships are illustrated in the following formula. The attenuation constant of the air, which changes depending on sound frequency, air temperature and relative humidity, exceeds the scope of this book.

Overall equivalent absorption area of a room

$$A_{tot} = \sum_{i=1}^{n} \alpha_i \cdot S_i + A_{fur} + A_{pers} \left[m^2 \right]$$

with A_{tot} Overall equivalent absorption area of a room [m^2]
 α_i Sound absorption coefficient i [-]
 S_i Surface in question, facing the room i [m^2]
 A_{fur} Absorption area of the furnishings in a room [m^2]
 A_{pers} Absorption area of the people in a room [m^2]

The overall equivalent absorption area A_{tot} together with the room volume can be used to determine the reverberation time T according to Sabine's law of reverberation, developed by US American physicist Wallace Clement Sabine (1868–1919) in 1898, which specifies the reverberance of a room:

Sabine's law of reverberation of the reverberation time T

$$T = 0{,}163 \cdot \frac{V}{A_{tot}} \, [s]$$

with T   Reverberation time [s]
 V   Room volume [m^3]
 A_{tot} Overall equivalent absorption area
   of a room [m^2]

Reverberation time describes how many seconds it takes for the diffuse sound pressure level to drop by 60 dB, from the moment the sound source is no longer active. Thus, in practice, reverberation time is an important parameter because the equivalent absorption areas of materials, construction elements and rooms can be measured by rearranging the formula, in order to determine the sound absorption coefficient of each object. The sound absorbers necessary inside a room can be determined in the same manner to achieve the desired reverberation time for different requirements. This is important, since reverberation time is a critical room acoustics factor for audibility in auditoria or for the musical impression in concert halls. Everyone who has clapped hands in a room before and after removing all of the items, during a move, for example, knows how strongly the reverberance of a room depends on the sound-absorbing surfaces in the room. The more absorptive surfaces there are, the 'dryer' the acoustics.

In addition to audibility, the sound pressure level distribution plays an important role in evaluating the acoustics of a room. Hereby, we differentiate between direct and diffuse sound. Direct sound is that share of a sound field that reaches our ear without reflection and before the diffuse share of the sound field. Direct sound lets the human ear perceive the direction of a sound source. If the sound source lies within line of sight, direct sound determines the understandability and the individual impression of volume.

As soon as direct sound hits an object in the room, it is reflected, and we speak of diffuse sound. This share of sound reaches our ear later than direct sound; due to the reflection and the longer path it takes it has less energy and is therefore less understandable. The reflections also mean that human hearing assumes the sound source coming from a different direction than is actually the case. The border between direct and diffuse sound is called reverberation radius, with the zero-point lying at the sound source. If diffuse sound is absorbed by absorption measures, the reverberation radius grows. If no absorption measures are taken, so-called flutter echoes can occur between parallel construction elements. These flutter echoes are generated because the sound waves keep oscillating or are being reflected between parallel walls/ceilings for a longer period of time. This phenomenon is easily explicable with the fact that sound energy striking a level plane is reflected according to the principle of 'angle of incidence equal to angle of emergence'.

SUMMARY ACOUSTICS AND TYPICAL WALL CONSTRUCTIONS

Sound energy is transmitted via the movement of molecules. Hereby, the movements in gases and liquids differ from those in solid matter by their different molecular arrangement: molecules in solid matter are elastically connected. Molecules in gases and liquids are a very different matter – here, the molecules are not connected. Therefore, the sound-insulating property of a building construction largely depends on whether it is subjected to airborne or solid-borne sound. In case of an excitation via solid-borne sound, the building construction acts like an amplifier (classic example: putting an ear on a railway track) – contrary to excitation via airborne sound. If the frequency of the incident airborne sound waves is not close to the natural frequency of the construction element, airborne sound is transformed into solid-borne sound when striking the construction element, but the sound energy is immediately weakened by reflection and dissipation. The absorptivity of individual building materials mainly depends on their area-related mass (raw density [kg/m³] times thickness [m²]). However, sound absorption is also influenced by the molecular structure of the material. This statement can be illustrated with the following wall constructions → **16–19.**

A single-shell exterior wall construction is subjected to airborne sound on the inside and the outside. When striking a construction element surface, a share of the sound energy is reflected. The remaining sound pressure is transmitted via solid-borne sound, i.e. molecular movement inside the construction element. Transmission takes place via all available areas; that means including adjacent construction elements and ceilings. During transmission, the sound pressure loses more and more energy until the solid-borne sound is again radiated from the construction element surface in the form of airborne sound. If the frequency of the incident airborne sound wave and the natural frequency of the construction element are approximately the same, the sound energy is transmitted through the construction element almost unchanged via solid-borne sound, because the resonance of the construction element continues to build up by the resulting resonance. In the case of a single-shell construction the worst scenario is a resonance catastrophe; i.e. the construction element is destroyed.

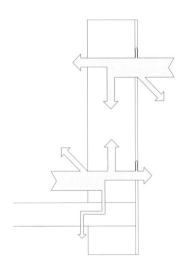

16

Schematic section through a single-shell wall construction
The surface of a construction element reflects a share of the sound energy.

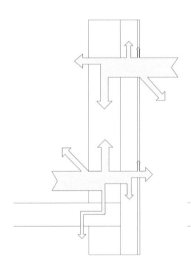

17

Schematic section through a wall construction with exterior insulation
A 'hard' insulation such as EPS dissipates sound only to a small degree.

With double-shell constructions, a 'spring' in the system prevents such resonance catastrophes. One typical example is a single-shell exterior wall construction with interior or exterior insulation → **17+18**; in terms of building physics, this constitutes a mass-spring-mass system (also valid for massive ceilings). The insulation acts as a spring that connects the shells (wall and plaster) elastically. An air layer as well as an insulation layer can act as a spring. In order to achieve the best possible sound absorption, the spring's dynamic rigidity (spring rigidity) should be as low as possible. Hereby, dynamic rigidity mainly depends on the molecular structure of the material, i.e. the dynamic elasticity modulus.

If the excitation frequency of the incident sound wave is above the natural frequency of the double-shell construction elements, the sound-insulating property of a double- or multi-shell construction element is significantly higher than that of a single-shell construction element. This is because the insulation in the first shell cannot vibrate in phase with the second shell due to the spring effect of the insulation.

The example of an insulated exterior wall construction (mineral fibre) with rear-ventilated façade → **19** illustrates that the resilience of the insulation largely depends on its molecular structure. The fibrous molecular structure dissipates significantly more sound energy than a 'hard' insulation such as EPS (expanded polystyrene), for example. Since room acoustics is mainly influenced by the material surfaces of the construction elements in a room, they must be selected carefully. Sound energy must be purposefully reflected and absorbed/dissipated by these materials in order to achieve good audibility and sound quality.

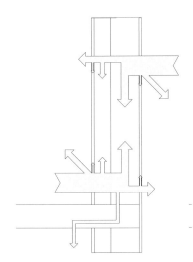

18

Schematic section through a wall construction with interior insulation
The effect of interior insulation is determined by its materiality.

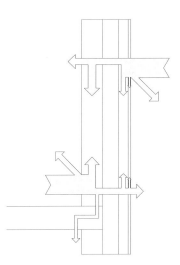

19

Schematic section through a rear-ventilated wall construction
The resilience of the mineral fibre insulation is determined by its molecular structure.

6 Light

Daylight and artificial lighting have a psychological impact on human beings, and solar gains can have a positive or negative influence on the room climate. Individual work performance and general sense of well-being are impacted as well. The deciding factors are luminous flux, luminance intensity, light intensity, luminous density as well as luminous colour. In parallel, the essential influencing variables concerning solar gains, i.e. heating of the space, are share of window area, storage mass, local climate and sun protection. Daylight in interior spaces is considered a necessity for the human sense of comfort because it allows us to visually perceive the dynamic course of the day and changing seasons → **1**. However, possible disadvantages are excessive heating due to intensive solar gains as well as glaring due to direct solar incidence – the greater the transparent share of a façade and the more window areas are oriented toward the south, the more perceptible these disadvantages are.

PRINCIPLES

Light is the share of electromagnetic radiation originating from a light source that is visible to the human eye and whose wavelengths lie between 380 nm and 780 nm. At wavelengths of 380 nm, human colour perception senses a violet colour space, which, based on the spectral colours, flows smoothly toward a wavelength of 780 nm into the colour space red. The adjacent areas are called ultraviolet and infrared radiation → **2**.

Since the transitions between these electromagnetic spectra are smooth and depend on the individual sensitivity of the human eye, these invisible areas are often also called light. Even though UV and IR radiation does not lie in the visible wavelength range, they can exert influence on our bodies. Examples are UV radiation causing sunburn (erythema) and pigmentary abnormalities, as well as an increased risk of pinkeye (conjunctivitis). The main impact that IR radiation has on human beings is the body heating beyond the limits of comfort.

1

Cupola of the Pantheon, Rome, ca. 125 B.C.E.
Besides the entrance, a circular aperture at the apex of the cupola is the only light source for the interior space.

The human eye can adapt to different levels of brightness. Our maximum eye sensitivity shifts to another wavelength range, depending on day or night brightness → **3**. With daylight, the maximum sensitivity is in the wave range of 555 nm (colour sensation yellow-green), and the eye is approximately 20 times more sensitive to these colours as to blue (450 nm) or red (670 nm). The sensitivity of an eye that is adapted to darkness lies in the wavelength range of 507 nm (colour sensation blue-green).

In summary, it can be derived that the wavelength spectrum between 380 and 780 nm as well as the brightness perception of the human eye, dependent on the ambient lighting, are critical factors for our sense of perception. Photometric values are derived based on this knowledge. These are measurable values that consider the sensitivity of the viewer.

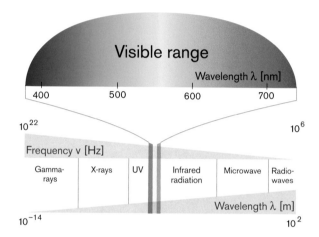

2

Wavelength spectrum of the visible range of light originating from a light source
The graph shows the entire wavelength spectrum of electromagnetic radiation. The visible share of electromagnetic radiation, i.e. the visible light, is in the range of 380 nm (violet) to 780 nm (red).

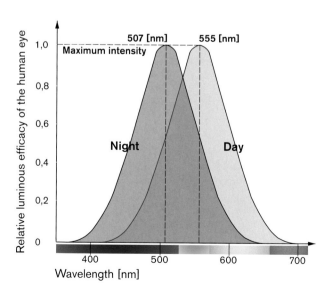

3

Maximum intensity of day and night brightness
The maximum intensity of day and night brightness describes the human perception of colours (wavelengths) at different times of the day. During daytime, yellow light is perceived as brighter than red light, even at equal intensities. With scotopic vision (low light conditions), the sensitivity of the eye shifts by about 50 nm into the shorter-wave, blue range. Shades of blue therefore appear brighter than during daytime. This is the reason why blue lights, such as Xenon automotive headlights, appear brighter during night.

PHOTOMETRIC PARAMETERS

Colour temperature or luminous colour K (Kelvin) is a reference value to quantitatively define the colour impression of a light source. Herefore, an ideal black body (according to Planck's law of radiation and Wien's displacement law) is set in an intensity curve to describe the maximum intensity of a body. This maximum defines in which wavelength spectrum the turning point lies, or which wavelength and therefore colour is perceived the strongest at which temperature, and in which wavelength spectra they are. This can be done by heating a thermal radiator (black radiator), which acts as a radiation source, based on a temperature of 0 K (−237 °C). The electromagnetic energy of the thermal radiation emitted from the black body is a mix of electromagnetic waves of a broad wavelength spectrum. The higher the temperature of the black radiator, the more the maximum intensity shifts toward shorter wavelengths (colour sensation blue-green). Thus, the higher the temperature of a body, the bluer is its colouring.

This can be observed in a dimmed glow filament of a halogen lamp (colour temperature 2700−3000 K): in the dimmed (colder) range the filament glows red, at higher temperature it glows orange to yellowish-white. In addition, the efficiency of a light source → 4 can be determined. Exceptions are RGB-LEDs as well as coloured glass plates of light sources. If the apex lies within the maximum intensity of the visible range (daylight brightness, wave band 555 nm), an effective use of the light source can be basically assumed (sunlight approximately 5000−5900 K) → 5. If the radiation maximum of a light source such as a common light bulb (2600−2800 K) is within the IR radiation band (infrared), thermal radiation predominates. The radiation power of a traditional 100 Watt light bulb is divided in 0.03 Watt in the UV radiation range (ultraviolet radiation) and 84 Watt in the IR radiation range. Only 9 Watt radiation power lies within the visual radiation range (total radiation power 93 Watt) – meaning that, on average, only 5 % of the energy input are transformed into 'light'.

Therefore, considering energy savings, the incremental light bulb ban introduced by the EU in 2009 makes sense. In short, luminous colour consists of individual spectral colours of specific wavelengths, and describes the colour impression of a light source. It should not be confused with the colour impression of the light reflected from a lit body (non-luminous colour).

4

Radiation spectra for different temperatures
Radiation intensity of a black radiator at different temperatures. The lower the temperature of the black radiator, the more the maximum intensity lies in the red range of the radiation spectrum, and the higher the temperature, the more the radiation intensity shifts toward the violet range. The spectral intensity distribution of a light source should cover the entire colour space in order to achieve an optimum colour representation.

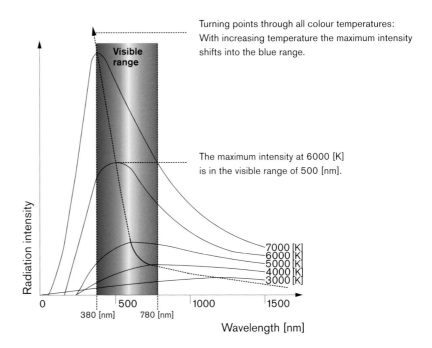

Turning points through all colour temperatures: With increasing temperature the maximum intensity shifts into the blue range.

The maximum intensity at 6000 [K] is in the visible range of 500 [nm].

The total visible light efficiency of a light source in a room (colloquially 'light') is called luminous flux (Φ_v lumen, short: lm). The unit lm is mainly used for classification purposes and to compare light sources.

However, the so-called luminous efficacy (η lm/W) provides a qualitative statement about the efficiency of an illuminant. In order to determine luminous efficacy, the visible light (Lumen) is divided by the maximum electrical power input (Watt). The higher this value, the greater the luminous efficacy or the efficiency of the light source.

Under inclusion of the solid angle (steradian, sr), luminous flux (Lumen) results in light intensity candela (cd) → **6+7**. The solid angle (Ω) is an essential parameter in lighting technology → **8**. It is used to determine quantitative statements such as emission quantity of a light source into the room or onto a surface.

The entire light (luminous flux) emitted from a light source radiates in different directions depending on how the beams are focussed and on the type of lighting fixture. Light intensity candela describes the share of the luminous flux that is emitted in a certain direction in the room as well as the maximum light range → **10+11**. Candela is derived from the Latin term for candle. A traditional wax candle has a light intensity of 1 candela (cd).

Luminous colour	Colour temperature [Kelvin]
Warm white	< 3300 K
Neutral white	3300–5300 K
Daylight white	> 5300 K
Light source	**Standard colour temperature [Kelvin]**
Candle	1000 K
Light bulb	2600 K
Halogen lamp	3400 K
Fluorescent lamp	2700–8000 K
LED lamp	1000–7000 K
Sunshine	6000 K
Sky (clear)	10,000 K

5

Luminous colour groups per light source
The table shows different standard values of the colour temperatures for commercially available light sources. It indicates which light source is suited for which application.

6

Schematic representation of luminous flux
Luminous flux is the total light efficiency of a light source.

Light source	Luminous flux [Lumen]	Luminous efficacy [lm/W]
Candlelight	15 lm	0.1 to 0.2 lm/W
Light bulb (60 W)	810 lm	13.5 lm/W
Light bulb (100 W)	1500 lm	15 lm/W
Halogen lamp (35 W)	600 lm	17 lm/W
Halogen lamp (75 W)	1600 lm	21.3 lm/W
Energy-saving lamp (15 W)	900 lm	60 lm/W
Fluorescent lamp (23 W)	1500 lm	65.2 lm/W
LED light (20 W)	2300 lm	115 lm/W

7

Luminous efficacy of different light sources
The efficiency of a lamp is called luminous efficacy.

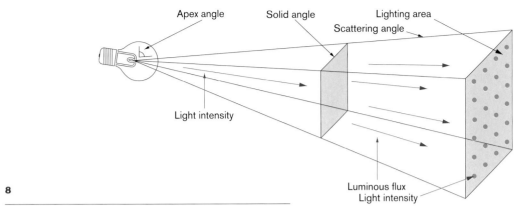

8

Schematic representation of the solid angles
The solid angle is used to determine the emission quantity of a
light source.

Apex angle [α]	Solid angle [Ω]	Apex angle [α]	Solid angle [Ω]
1°	0.000239 sr	65.541°	1 sr
5°	0.00598 sr	90°	1.840 sr
10°	0.0239 sr	120°	(2π =) 3.142 sr
30°	0.214 sr	180°	(3π =) 6.283 sr
45°	0.478 sr	270°	10.726 sr
60°	0.842 sr	360°	(4π =) 12.566 sr

9

Overview of common solid angles
Comparison between different apex angles and solid angles.

10

Schematic representation of light intensity
A share of the luminous flux that is emitted in a certain direction
is defined via the light intensity.

Light source	Light intensity [candela]
Candle flame	1 cd
Light bulb (60 W)	ca. 60 cd
Light bulb (100 W)	ca. 120 cd
Fluorescent lamp (40 W)	ca. 180 cd
Full beam (automobile) max. value	225,000 cd
Sun	ca. $3*10^{27}$ cd

11

Light intensities of different light sources
Comparison of the light intensities of different typical light sources.

Light conditions (outside)	Luminance intensity [lux]
Sky (summer, sunny)	ca. 100,000 lx
Sky (summer, no sunlight)	ca. 50,000 lx
Sky (summer, cloud cover)	ca. 20,000 lx
Sky (winter, sunny)	ca. 20,000 lx
Sky (winter, cloud cover)	ca. 5000 lx
Full moon	ca. 0,25 lx
Work area (inside)	**Luminance intensity [lux]**
Circulation area, hallways, stairs, lifts	100 lx (required)
Gymnasiums, swimming pools	300 lx (required)
Office work place	500 lx (required)
Medical examination and treatment rooms	1000 lx (required)
Operating theatres	10,000 lx (required)

12

Light conditions of different light sources
The luminance intensity of all natural light conditions and the standard requirements for work areas can be used to determine which measures should be taken to create optimum luminance intensities for work spaces.

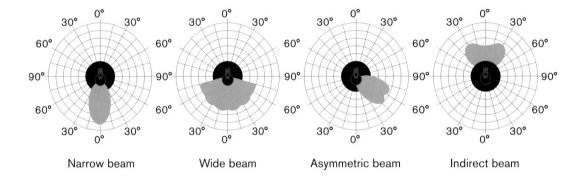

Narrow beam   Wide beam   Asymmetric beam   Indirect beam

13

Light intensity distribution curves for different light sources
Light intensity distribution curves can be specified for any lamp, which describes it light intensity for various angles.

Therefore, light intensity is the maximum strength illuminating a point from a distance of 1 m (laboratory conditions). Usually, these values are stated on illuminants as well as lamps in the form of a graphic light intensity distribution curve (polar diagram) → **13**.

This is different for the luminance intensity lux (lx). Whereas light intensity candela defines the luminous flux related to the solid angle and the maximum strength in one point, luminance intensity lux relates to a reference area, i.e. the luminous flux lumen per unit area m².

Thus, luminance intensity is the measurement of the amount of light striking a surface (1 lux = 1 Lm/m²). The farther the distance from a light source to an object, the weaker the luminance intensity, whereby the luminous flux remains constant → **14+15**. This means that luminance intensity is a receiving value, serving as a measurement for brightness. Luminance intensity is a relevant parameter in lighting technology; it is also part of the standard requirements for work areas → **16**.

The prescribed minimum requirement for light and lighting of work areas (according to DIN EN 12464-1:2011-08) depends on the visual tasks in a particular work area → **12**.

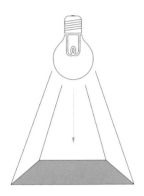

14

Schematic representation of luminance intensity
The amount of light striking a surface is called luminance intensity.

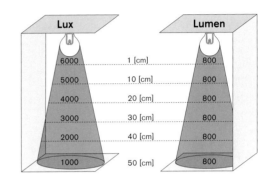

15

Lux vs. lumen
Light intensity refers to the maximum strength of the luminous flux in one point, while luminance intensity describes the amount of light on a surface.

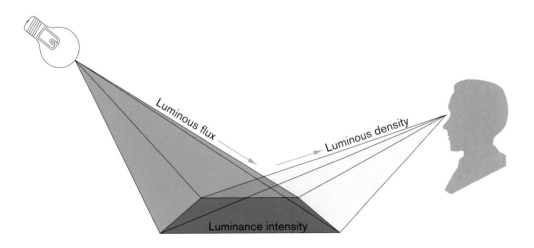

16

Schematic representation of luminous density
The impression of brightness of an illuminating or reflecting surface on the human eye is called luminous density; it can be specified mathematically.

Luminous density or luminance (L) is the physical measurement unit for the impression of brightness that the human eye can sense from an illuminated, illuminating or reflecting surface → **17**. Luminance makes it possible to define the perceived impression of brightness of a light source (colour, contrast, brightness) as a mathematically tangible value.

Therefore, luminous density is the photometric parameter that conveys a direct relationship with the optical sensation.

The impression of brightness depends on the directly lit surface (colouring, surface properties) or an indirectly lit surface (lit by radiation, emission, transmission) as well as their solid angle (angle of light source, viewing angle) → **18**. A white sheet of paper, for example, in an office work place with the required luminance intensity of 500 lux, features a luminous density of 100 cd/m². In short, it can be stated that a light source is perceived as the brighter, the greater the emitted luminous flux or the smaller the emitting surface.

Light conditions (outside)	Luminous density [L]
Sun at its zenith, clear sky	1,600,000,000 cd/m²
Blue sky, midday	8000 cd/m²
Overcast sky, midday	2000 cd/m²
Night sky	0,01 cd/m²
Light source (inside)	**Luminous density [L]**
LED (white)	500,000,000 cd/m²
Light bulb, clear	10,000,000 cd/m²
Light bulb, matt	2,000,000 cd/m²
Fluorescent lamp	70,000 cd/m²
White sheet of paper (at 500 lx)	100 cd/m²
Candle flame	0.75 cd/m²

17

Luminous density of different light sources
Comparison of natural light conditions and light sources concerning their luminous density.

18

Overview of photometric values
Summarising overview of all mentioned photometric values.

Solid angle	Luminous flux	Luminance intensity
Solid angle/steradian SI unit: Omega [sr] Symbol: Ω	Luminous flux SI unit: Lumen [lm] Symbol: Φ	Luminance intensity SI unit: Lux [lx] Symbol: M
$1\,sr = \dfrac{1\,m^2}{1\,m^2}$	$1\,lm = 1\,cd * 1\,sr$	$1\,lx = \dfrac{1\,lm}{1\,m^2}$
$\Omega = \dfrac{A}{r^2}$ [in sr]	$\Phi = L * \Omega$ [in lm]	$E = \dfrac{\Omega}{A}$ [in lx] for point-like light sources $E = \dfrac{I}{r^2}$ [in lx]

COMPARISON OF DAYLIGHT AND ARTIFICIAL LIGHT

Per definition, daylight is understood as the visible light of the sun over the course of the day, from sunrise to sunset. It is scientifically proven that daylight has a positive effect on the human being, physically as well as psychologically. The experience of the dynamic change of the time of day and time of year as well as the sensation of weather changes, even perceived through the windows from the inside of a building, has a strong influence on the sense of well-being of the human organism. It stimulates vitamin formation, strengthens the body's defences, controls metabolism and hormonal balance, and verifiably increases work performance at work places. Furthermore, optimally used daylight reduces the energy demand for lighting. The luminance intensity of natural light fluctuates between 5000 lux (winter) and 20,000 lux (summer) depending on the weather, daytime and season.

Contrary to natural light, artificial light emitted by an illuminant has a static effect on human beings. Artificial light always means that electrical energy is needed, and, depending on the intensity of the IR radiation, it contributes to the building heating up (additional heat gain). Today, it is technically possible to simulate the course of the sun with lighting control systems. But the illuminant chosen determines the static luminous colour of the artificial light, which in itself does not convey any change over the course of the day. In principle, people generally perceive natural sunlight as more pleasant and more valuable than artificial light. Therefore, artificial light cannot be compared with the totality of the sunlight. Natural light displays the entire range of spectral colours, which represents the true colours of items a lot more precisely than artificial light does.

Independent hereof, artificial light can be used very specifically considering the maximum intensity of its luminous colour. Supermarkets can, for example, use certain luminous colours to specifically enhance the perceived colour of food such as fruit, vegetables or meat, to make them look fresh and appealing. In museums, particularly fine art museums, exhibits can be optimally staged with artificial light, but it can also be used to protect the exhibits from 'harmful' UV light. Other fields where artificial light can be employed advantageously are medicine (light therapy), plant and animal breeding, automotive lighting and photography.

Lux vs. lumen	Light intensity	Luminous density
Luminous efficacy – $\eta = \dfrac{\Phi}{P}$ [in lm/W] Electrical power – Unit: Watt [W] Symbol: P Area (distance) – Unit: [m²] Symbol: A Viewed surface – Unit: [m²] Symbol: A_p	Light intensity SI unit: Candela [cd] Symbol: I	Luminous density SI unit: Candela [cd/m²] Symbol: L
	$1\,cd = \dfrac{1\,lm}{1\,sr}$	$1\,L = \dfrac{1\,cd}{1\,m^2}$
	$I = \dfrac{\Phi}{\Omega}$ [in cd]	$L = \dfrac{I}{A_p}$ [in sr]

Visual comfort

Comfort is a term describing the physical and emotional condition of a subjective sense of well-being. The sense of well-being can be deliberately influenced or improved with appropriate lighting concepts → **19+20, 22**, amongst other things. As mentioned earlier, daylight acts more dynamically in terms of changing light intensity, and thereby conveys a sensation of the time of day and weather conditions, and it allows for better colour representation. As important is the visual connection with the outside world, not least to cater to the natural escape reflex of human beings. Hereby, optimum layout (high position) and size are essential. According to modern standards, the light area (window size) must account for at least 10% of the footprint of the room; increased visual comfort, however, requires a light area of around 20 to 30% of the footprint. Window height should be chosen such that a permanent visual connection to the outside world is granted without glaring. Another factor to consider is that the changing angle of incident light limits the intensity of the daylight that enters the room. This decreasing luminance intensity should be balanced with appropriate artificial light or light-directing measures.

And a temperature increase caused by solar radiation must be taken into account – the larger the windows, the stronger this effect is; in the case of office buildings, it can quickly result in overheating of the interior. Temporary overheating can be addressed with active cooling, high storage masses in the building (heavy construction elements, massive construction) as well as efficient shading.

19

VitraHaus, Weil am Rhein, Herzog & de Meuron, 2009
Interior room with maximum visual connection to the outside world.
An interior sun protection system prevents direct glare.

20

Zollverein School of Management and Design, Essen, Sanaa, 2006
Indoor room of the school building. The layout of the windows on the southwest and northeast sides was oriented on the user requirements according to a daylight analysis (e.g. computer work place, seminar room).

The prevention of direct glare as well as of glare by reflection (indirect glare) is an important aspect for visual comfort → **21**. Long-term glare leads to fatigue and headache. Direct glare results from a light source that is positioned in the direct field of vision, or from an excessive lighting contrast between a work space and the surrounding area; the latter case can usually be prevented with homogenous lighting of the entire room. Glare by reflection or indirect glare results from excessive reflection from surfaces such as walls or furniture. If light from a strong light source is reflected from a mirror surface, the luminous density can cause indirect glare. Such glare by reflection also occurs if, for example, monitors at work places are not positioned correctly.

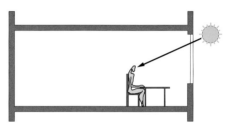

Direct glare

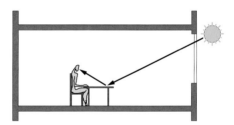

Glare by reflection/indirect glare

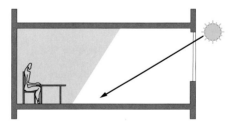

Glare caused by extreme lighting contrast

21

Types of glare
One important factor of visual comfort at the work place is to prevent direct and/or indirect glare.

Luminous density is a photometric parameter that has immediate relevance for the visual perception of the human eye. Luminance intensity in itself cannot be sensed; it becomes apparent in combination with material surfaces that exhibit different properties. Homogenously distributed luminous density that prevents reflections from shiny surfaces, for example on work tables, creates a comfortable visual environment.

In summarising, the essential indicators or quality criteria for sustained visual comfort include:
- visual connection with the outside,
- sufficient daylight,
- the level of lighting,
- luminous density distribution,
- prevention of glare effects and reflections by natural as well as artificial light,
- light direction and shading,
- luminous colour as well as
- colour rendering or colour trueness of objects and surfaces.

Daylight in interior spaces

In terms of standards, daylight in interior spaces can be examined and evaluated from different points of view:
- psychological effect (e.g. DIN 5034 – Daylight in interiors, DIN EN 12464 – Light and lighting),
- viewing conditions (e.g. DIN EN 12464 – Light and lighting),
- biological effects (DIN EN 12464 – Light and lighting),
- thermal comfort (DIN EN ISO 7730 – Ergonomics of the thermal environment), and
- energy efficiency (DIN V 18599 – Energy efficiency of buildings, DIN EN 15193 – Energy requirements for lighting).

The psychological effect comprises the subjective perception of brightness as well as the necessary visual connection with the outside world. The optimum visual conditions refer to appropriate luminance intensity, depending on the viewing task or the task to be executed. Reducing glare also belongs to this category. Biological comfort includes a general sense of comfort, health as well as possible performance enhancement. It is not yet normatively defined in standards and regulations, even though those works refer to it. Thermal comfort is indirectly linked to biological comfort. It deals with restricting solar radiation and heating, which can also lead to discomfort. Lastly, energy efficiency must be considered: it describes the reduction of the energy demand in buildings by a dedicated use of daylight.

It should be noted that these standards regulate only minimum requirements (for habitable rooms). During planning, the normative daylight evaluation (DIN 5034) should be used to guarantee sufficient lighting in a building. Other resources are the daylight evaluations by building authorities or building certification systems (DGNB, LEED, BREEAM) as well as physically correct light simulation with appropriate software.

Normatively, the minimum requirements for daylight supply in interiors can be calculated with the daylight coefficient (D, daylight factor). Simply put, it describes the relationship between luminance intensity E_p in interiors, measured at a point at windowsill height, and luminance intensity E_a in the exterior, measured under conditions of an open, unobstructed hemisphere and overcast sky. This results in the percentage of daylight at any random point in the room. The daylight coefficient is a planning aid for possible room dimensioning, including the number and size of necessary window openings as well as the choice of glazing.

22

Jacob-und-Wilhelm-Grimm-Zentrum, Berlin, Max Dudler Architekten, 2009
The lighting of the terrace-like, sloped work areas of this university library is achieved by skylights.
Thus, direct glare is prevented.

The daylight coefficient is composed of:
- the sum of the share of skylight D_H, i.e. the share at reference point P,
- the share of interior reflection D_R, i.e. the share of sunlight that, on indoor surfaces, falls on reference point P by reflection,
- the share of exterior reflection D_V, i.e. the share of sunlight that falls on reference point P by reflection from neighbouring buildings, as well as
- the reduction factors kn, such as caused by frames and lattices, contamination or reduction related to the type of glazing.

The reference points P1, P2 should be set at half room depth at a height of 0.85 m above the floor and each 1 m away from the side walls. Averaged for both reference points, the minimum requirement of the daylight coefficient should be at least 0.9 % or at least 0.75 % at one of the points. To optimise light distribution and minimise possible direct glare, walls, ceilings and floor should be highly reflective, without creating glare by reflection, however → **23**.

The daylight coefficient D therefore is a parameter that is influenced by:
- room dimensions,
- number and size of apertures and their position,
- dimensions of construction elements,
- type of glazing,
- degree of reflection of the glazing, as well as
- walls, floor and ceiling.

All these parameters must be carefully considered in the design phase → **24**. One consideration during planning should be that later modifications of the window openings during the construction stage entail high expenditures in cost and labour, and could significantly change the appearance of the building.

23

Incident light related to room depth
Lighting a room with daylight is dependent of room depth and size of the apertures.

Global solar radiation

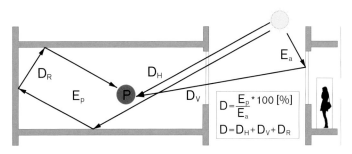

$$D = \frac{E_p}{E_a} * 100 \ [\%]$$

$$D = D_H + D_V + D_R$$

24

Schematic representation of the shares of the daylight coefficient
The daylight coefficient describes the minimum requirements for daylight supply. It is composed of room dimensions, apertures, construction elements, type of glazing and reflections.

SUN PROTECTION AND GLARE PROTECTION

For most living and work spaces, exploiting daylight for lighting requires the installation of a sun protection system that reduces solar incidence when necessary. The essential parameters for the calculation of solar incidence are the solar factor (solar transmittance) g of the glazing and the reduction factor F_c of the sun protection system. The chosen sun protection system must ensure that – depending on the use of the space – sufficient daylight enters the room, without requiring unnecessary use of artificial light. Besides economic factors, the parameters for selecting a sun protection system are:

- expected weather conditions,
- orientation,
- degree of transparency of the façade, as well as
- optimum amount of daylight for the use of the room while maintaining maximum user comfort.

Optimally, a sun protection system should direct daylight into the room such that no occupant is subjected to glare. Excessive solar incidence in summer should be avoided, whereas maximum values are desirable in winter.

There is a principal distinction between interior and exterior sun protection system → **25 + 26**, and there are solutions that feature sun protection inside the gap between insulating glazing panes.

A sun protection system can work in different ways: based on reflection, absorption, reduction, selection or transformation → **28**. Depending on the material, Venetian blinds can reflect and/or absorb sunlight. Horizontal projections like balconies and awnings only absorb. Printed glazing or exterior structured panels made of various materials can reduce solar incidence. Solar glazing admits light selectively; translucent glass disperses solar radiation and thus transforms it.

Exterior sun protection systems are usually up to five times more effective than those mounted on the inside, yet significantly more expensive. Another aspect to consider is that flexible systems such as awnings or blinds might have to be retracted during strong winds, thereby nullifying glare protection. This problem does not apply to stiff sliding systems or rigid, horizontal projections. The reduction factor F_c of an exterior sun protection system can be up to 0.1.

In contrast, interior systems only reach a maximum of 0.3. Interior systems reflect the sunlight onto the glazing, which is why their effectiveness partially depends on the properties of the glazing. Glare protection should be noted in this context, even though it does not prevent solar radiation heating up the room. A compromise are sun protection systems inside the gap between glazing panes → **27** in the form of fixed intermediate layers, prints or louvres, the latter also being available in adjustable form. The disadvantages of such systems are high cost and the risk in case of defects, since the entire system including glazing must be exchanged. With these systems, the solar factor of the glazing can be reduced to a maximum of 0.15 → **29**.

25

Interior sun protection system
VitraHaus, Weil am Rhein, Herzog & de Meuron, 2009, is equipped with an interior sun protection system.

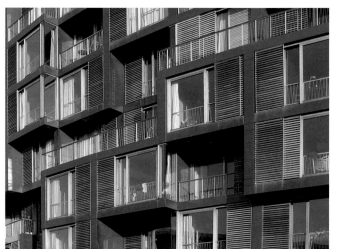

26

Exterior sun protection system
Tietgen Student Housing, Copenhagen, Lundgaard & Tranberg Architects, 2007, has an exterior sun protection system.

27

**Sun protection system in the gap between the glazing panes,
research project ETA-Fabrik, Darmstadt Technical University, 2016**
Close-up of a sun protection system in the gap between panes.

Glare protection is employed to keep the luminous density difference in the room as low as possible, and to ensure that no direct sunlight and/or reflections impair the user. However, sufficient daylight should be allowed into the room, for example, by installing Venetian blinds or roller blinds that can be moved in both directions, i.e. also from the bottom upward. This means that daylight could still fall into the room through the upper part of the window, while the protection in the lower part prevents glare in the work place area. Another option are films on the glazing, which, just like bidirectional blinds, allow for visual contact with the outside.

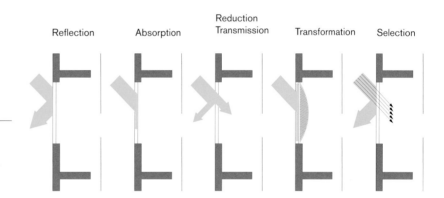

28

Mode of operation of sun protection systems
A sun protection system must be adapted to the ambient conditions and the requirements of the type of use of the indoor space.

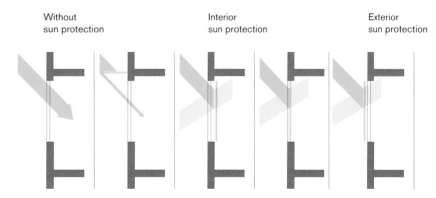

29

Overview sun protection
Comparison of different types and positions of sun protection.

DAYLIGHT-DIRECTING SYSTEMS

Daylight directing can significantly increase the user comfort level in indoor spaces → **31**. There are systems that diffuse daylight, and systems that exploit it by targeted redirection → **30**. Daylight directing makes it possible that daylight reaches deep into the back areas of the room, thus reducing the demand for artificial light. Daylight directing automatically includes glare protection. Just like sun protection systems, daylight directing systems can be installed on the outside, the inside and in the gap between panes.

The systems also differ in whether they transport direct or diffuse light, and in whether they are static or adjustable. Some adjustable systems even use motor-driven controls to follow the path of the daylight in order to increase efficiency. In both cases, the light is directed into the room via the ceiling. The ceiling should be as bright as possible with a reflection factor of up to 0.9. Additional reflective ceiling elements can further increase the light-directing effect.

Directing daylight into a building does achieve increased brightness but it also entails the risk of overheating. It is therefore recommended to combine light-directing systems with sun protection. This could be the addition of a bidirectional Venetian blind that serves as sun protection in the viewing area but lets light penetrate into the room in the upper part. Reflective surfaces on the façade could be exterior variants. More expensive are solutions that direct only light from certain angles into the room, while blocking energy-intensive radiation.

30

Daylight-directing system with integrated sun protection, AIT – Austrian Institute of Technology, ENERGYbase, Wien, POS Architecture, 2008
This example shows a daylight-directing system with integrated sun protection.

31

Daylight-directing system, SKF Solution Factory, Madrid, 2013
This daylight-directing system creates a diffuse light distribution of sunlight inside the room.

Diffuse daylight-directing systems reduce the risk of overheating. They are designed to optimally exploit otherwise insufficient amounts of daylight to light rear areas of indoor spaces. They are suitable for regions with few sunny days or, generally, on north-facing façades or densely built-up areas with extreme shading. Typically, diffuse light must be caught in front of the façade before being directed into the interior. Daylight can also be repeatedly reflected in light tubes, and thereby transported over long distances in order to light windowless rooms → **32**.

The light yield decreases meter by meter. For the sake of completeness, light diffusing systems should be noted; they were already mentioned earlier in connection with sun protection systems → **33**.

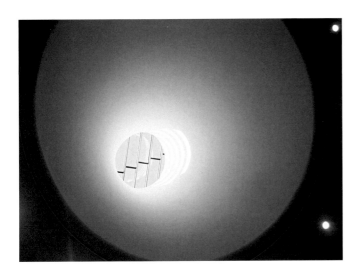

32

Targeted light directing through light tubes
Daylight light tubes direct daylight from the roof of a building to the interior.

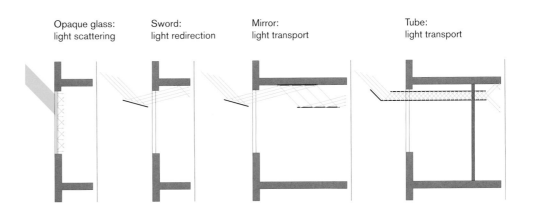

33

Selection of established light-directing systems
Different light-directing systems allow for better diffusion of natural light, or direct it to the back areas of the interior spaces.

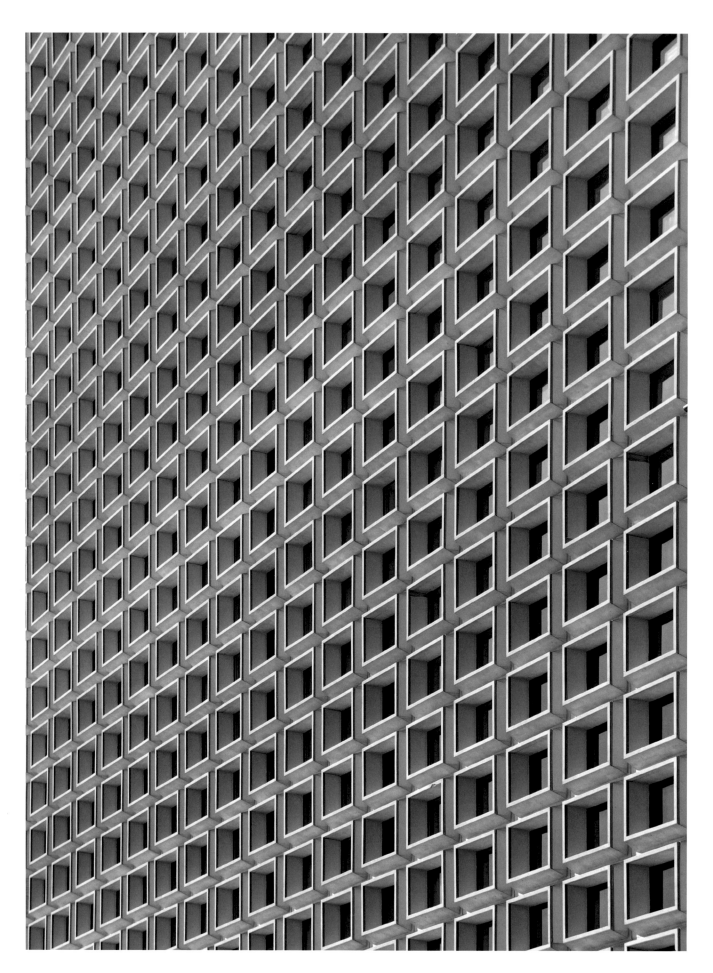

7 Building Physics in Practice

What does the application of the knowledge of building physics in daily building practice look like? What are the typical solutions to fulfil the multitude of requirements concerning the building envelope? And in what manner are the individual building elements joined into one construction?

To answer these questions, the building process of three conventional housing buildings was photographically documented to illustrate the construction details and make them comprehensible. Representing the typical construction types 'single-shell massive exterior wall construction', 'exterior wall with thermal insulation composite system' and 'rear-ventilated exterior wall construction' as discussed in chapters 2 'Thermal Energy', 3 'Moisture', 4 'Airtightness' and 5 'Acoustics', three projects were chosen due to their transferrable construction types. They were examined with regard to requirements concerning heat insulation, moisture protection, airtightness and sound protection; the solutions are illustrated here. The exterior wall construction with interior insulation is not treated here because it is usually exclusively used in renovation projects. Even though the three examples are residential buildings, the construction types can be applied to other uses as well.

The first example, a single-shell massive construction is a single-family home that was newly built in 2017 in Düsseldorf, Germany → **1**. The walls are constructed with aerated concrete blocks, covered with a plaster layer on the outside and the inside.

The project with a thermal insulation composite system is a multi-storey apartment building, also built in 2017 in Düsseldorf, Germany → **2**. The walls are made of poured concrete, covered with heat insulation on the outside, and a plaster layer on the inside.

Our third example, the rowhouses in Ouddorp in the Netherlands, were built in 2017 with prefabricated concrete parts, covered with an insulation layer and a rear-ventilated brick layer on the outside → **3**. In the interior, only parts of the walls were covered with a plaster layer, due to budget constraints.

Besides the actual construction of the three examples, the connection with the ground as well as the openings in the constructions in the form of window or door apertures are particularly interesting. These areas highlight the structural scheme and the functioning.

1

Single-family home Düsseldorf
Single-shell massive construction made of aerated concrete blocks.

2

Multi-family home in Düsseldorf
In situ poured concrete with thermal insulation
composite system.

3

Single-family rowhouses in Ouddorp
Rear-ventilated brick cladding in front of a construction made of prefabricated
concrete elements.

THERMAL INSULATION

Thermal insulation in a massive wall construction

The massive monolithic wall combines loadbearing and insulation functions in one construction element, which is why a massive building material with high porosity was chosen, in this case aerated concrete. This means that an uninterrupted wall area (no windows or doors) can achieve high insulation values with a very simple setup. This is supported by thin glued joints between the aerated concrete blocks since thicker mortar joints would exhibit greater heat conduction.

The various connection areas pose the highest risk of thermal bridges. The plinth area in → 4 shows that the opening wall protrudes out above the reinforced concrete base plate. As its higher density makes the base plate a good heat conductor, it is insulated in the lower area. The same principle is applied to the ceiling resting on the loadbearing wall, which is why it should not reach all the way to the outer edge of the aerated concrete blocks. Apertures such as shown in → 5 generally pose the risk of thermal bridges; therefore, insulation strips are often placed on the outside of the window reveal. In this regard, massive constructions offer uncomplicated connection possibilities.

Thermal insulation in a wall construction with thermal insulation composite system

The classic exterior wall construction with thermal insulation composite system separates the functions of loadbearing and insulation and they are fulfilled by the two characteristic layers; therefore, the transition needs to be carefully planned. The layering principle results in a very good insulating effect in the wall area, whereby reliable and waterproof plaster must be used in the case of insulation materials that are susceptible to moisture. Since the plaster is susceptible to cracking and can only be applied in very thin layers, a water-resistant insulation material is the safer option. The construction requires fastening elements or bonding glue. The first penetrate the insulation and thus create local thermal bridges. These can be reduced or avoided by minimising the size and number of fixtures.

5

Window connection in a single-shell construction
Window connection in the massive exterior wall of the single-family home. The image shows the installed window; the edge insulation of the ceiling is not installed yet.

4

Plinth area in a single-shell construction
Plinth area of the massive exterior wall of the single-family home. The image shows the base plate, with insulation layer in front of it and a plaster layer.

The detail in → **6** shows the insulation down to the base point; a water-resistant insulation material or top coat of plaster is mandatory. Insulation is also required where the base plate touches the ground, to avoid thermal bridges and to ensure protection against frost damage of the foundation. The interior loadbearing layer of the building ensures that the ceilings and walls are insulated. However, this also means that exterior installations and penetrations must be carefully executed.

The detail in → **7** shows that the window sits in the insulation, and that the window frame is thus predominantly held by a bracket. This setup counteracts possible thermal bridges in this area. Interruptions in the layers, such as the window sill, for example, create gaps in the insulation layer that need to be considered and sealed.

Thermal insulation in a rear-ventilated wall construction

With a rear-ventilated wall construction, all functions are distributed across the different layers, which results in a number of transitions and connections that must be carefully planned. Very good insulation properties can be achieved in uninterrupted wall areas even with more moisture-sensitive insulation materials because they are protected from direct rain and can easily dry due to the rear-ventilated structure. However, fastening elements are necessary for the insulation and the protective exterior façade. These elements can penetrate the insulation and, depending on their design, can cause local thermal bridges (for example, the steel bracket in → **7**). Minimising the size and number of such fastening elements can reduce or avoid thermal bridges.

6

Plinth area of wall construction with thermal insulation composite system
Base point of the concrete wall of the multi-family home.

7

Window joint of a wall construction with thermal insulation composite system
Window area of the multi-family home. The image shows the window, installed with the support of brackets.

In areas of possible moisture accumulation, the plinth area in → **8** shows the use of water-resistant insulation material to ensure the insulating effect close to the ground as well as in the splash water zone. Since the loadbearing layer is shifted to the innermost layer, the resulting geometry allows for insulating the ceilings. However, the many different layers pose demanding requirements on the detailing of the various connections.

This is illustrated by the window opening in → **9**. The interruption of the exterior wall construction for the window opening makes it necessary to merge the functions of the layers in the window area. This can lead to direct heat loss through the different connection joints if they are not sealed correctly. Care must be taken to create an interruption in highly conductive materials such as the metal window sills between the interior and the exterior, as was done in this example. Another problem can arise during the installation of soft insulation material, since it can settle easily and may no longer cover, as in this case, the upper area of the loadbearing inside wall. The rear ventilation would then cause cold outside air to reach the loadbearing wall surface, resulting in high heat loss.

8

Plinth area of a rear-ventilated wall construction
The base point of the single-family home is insulated with water-resistant insulation in the splash water zone.

9

Window connection in a rear-ventilated wall construction
Detail of the exterior wall of the single-family home with installed window.

MOISTURE PROTECTION

Moisture protection in a massive wall construction

With their thick building elements, massive, monolithic walls are easy to construct since there are few transitions to consider. Especially aerated concrete blocks, which are sanded during production and thus very flat and smooth, bear little risk of leakages since they are joined with thin glue joints. Exterior plaster protects the construction from driving rain.

Connections and transitions are the areas most prone to leakage. → **4** shows the base point of the single-family home, which, in the ground, is protected from pressing water with bitumen. Water-resistant insulation is installed in the area of the base plate, complemented by plaster and paint coating suited for the splash water zone. Apertures such as those in → **5** are also prone to leakage. With massive constructions, the low number of layers offers uncomplicated connection options, and there is little risk of joint fatigue. Sealing can be accomplished with polyurethane foam, for example, that is inserted into the gap between wall construction and window. Generally, the homogenous temperature distribution within the monolithic building element ensures minimal condensation issues.

Moisture protection in a wall construction with thermal insulation composite system

Separating the exterior wall construction with thermal insulation composite system into a massive loadbearing and a high-performance functional layer causes a temperature gradient across a short distance, which can lead to water condensation. This may not be too severe, and the moisture must be able to dissipate during evaporation periods. Hereby, the outer plaster layer must comply with weather protection requirements and guarantee long-term performance of the insulation layer. Good tightness can be achieved by closing off joints by overlapping. If fastening elements are used, care must be taken that there are no continuous paths for penetration and that the risk of localised condensation is minimised → **10 + 11**.

11

Window connection of wall construction with thermal insulation composite system
The exterior wall of the multi-family home with installed window.

10

Plinth area of wall construction with thermal insulation composite system
Base point of the loadbearing concrete wall of the multi-family home. The image shows the thermal insulation composite system as well as the protection against splash water.

The base point in → **10** shows the sealing measures in the splash and backed-up water areas: bitumen and foils. The insulation layer in the plinth area is also waterproof to prevent possible damage. All penetrations of the protective plaster layer must be executed very carefully to prevent water from entering the thermal insulation composite system.

The specific measures for sealing the window are careful plastering to the window frame and a well-conceived execution of the window sill → **11**. This is accomplished with sealing foils at the window and possibly behind the insulation, permanently secured with plaster netting. A permanently elastic joint completes the setup. The thermal insulation composite system is cut out to allow for the installation of the window sill and then sealed to prevent moisture from entering the wall.

Moisture protection in a rear-ventilated wall construction

In this rear-ventilated wall construction, all functions are distributed across the different layers. Similar to a rain jacket, the outer layer, for example, in the form of a separate clinker brick wall, provides protection against driving rain and splash water. If water still penetrates, the rear-ventilated construction (for example with open clinker brick joints) means that the water can drain or evaporate. However, with regard to air humidity, such an open construction must be planned in a way that loadbearing elements never come in contact with moisture. Especially joints between prefabricated parts and the use of a highly permeable insulation material pose the risk of water condensation. The insulation and the protective exterior façade are fastened with retaining elements. These also penetrate the insulation, and thus open up another path for water vapour and cold (see black fasteners in → **9**).

The different layers in the window area must be merged → **9**. The window can be joined with its sealing layer and with the sealing layer of the insulation by screwing the insulation to the loadbearing construction behind the rear-ventilated cladding.

The upper end of the building in → **12** shows that there many transitions between the loadbearing building elements for the roof, the insulation layers and the exterior shell. The roof construction comprises the foil underneath the roof battens, the roof tiles on top of these and the photovoltaic system, and therefore two sealing layers.

12

Upper end of the building of a rear-ventilated wall construction
The image shows the eave gutter detail above the façade of the single-family home.

AIRTIGHTNESS

Airtightness in a massive wall construction

Due to its thick building elements, a massive, monolithic construction is generally insusceptible to air leakages, particularly when common sanded, planar aerated concrete blocks are used. They are glued together and do not feature thick mortar joints. Even with installations in cable ducts that run along the interior surface, this construction type proves to be very airtight. If hollow bricks without filling are used, the risk of air leakage is greater when flush sockets and other interior installations are introduced. By accident, they can connect with the hollows in the bricks and then continuous air paths through the construction can ensue since the apertures in the bricks lie on top of each other. Even though this type of construction comprises very few layers and therefore does not benefit from one layer covering another to seal leakages, the construction shown in → **4+5** can be considered airtight.

Connections bear the greatest risk of leakages. → **13** shows the base point, which, if the base plate and connecting interior floor construction are well executed, should not pose any risk of leakage. Also, there are an additional sealing layer in the form of the exterior insulation of the base plate. Aperture details as those shown in → **5** are generally susceptible to leakages, but a massive construction method offers uncomplicated joint options and exhibits very little movement of the building elements that could lead to joint fatigue. Sealing can be accomplished with polyurethane foam.

Airtightness in a wall construction with thermal insulation composite system

The exterior wall construction with thermal insulation composite system consists of a loadbearing and a functional layer responsible for the insulating effect. An exterior plaster layer provides protection against weather. The layering method ensures high sealing performance by closing possible gaps and joints with overlapping elements. Even the crack-prone plaster adds to the airtightness, particularly if the insulation layer is glued on. If fastening elements are used, they penetrate the insulation and thus increase the risk of continuous paths through the wall.

The base point in → **14** is covered with insulation, which also ensures sealing of possible joint defects between the base plate and adjacent walls. The inner loadbearing layer in the entire building also provides for an insulation coverage of the ceilings and walls resting on the exterior wall, and therefore airtightness. All penetrations to the exterior must be carefully planned and executed.

13

Massive exterior wall
The aerated concrete wall sits on the ground floor slab; airtightness is ensured by the construction material and the mortar joints.

14

Window connection of the wall construction with thermal insulation composite system
Exterior wall detail of the multi-family home with installed and sealed window.

The aperture detail in → **14** shows that a very compact wall construction leaves little room for air leakages. The window frame is fastened to the ceiling with a steel bracket. Sealing foils mounted at the window can be used to create a sealing connection in the insulation layer, which reduces the permeability of joints and connections. The only problem can be the installation of the window sill because the thermal insulation composite system needs to be interrupted and sealed.

Airtightness in a rear-ventilated wall construction

In a rear-ventilated wall construction, the functions are distributed across the layers, resulting in a relatively high number of transitions and connections. The rear ventilation offers sufficient air supply in the outer layers. Airtightness must be achieved by connecting the outer and inner (loadbearing) layer to the loadbearing elements. Joints between prefabricated parts and highly permeable insulation material in particular are causes for leakages. The protective exterior façade requires fastening elements that also penetrate the insulation and thus allow for rear ventilation (see black fasteners in → **9**).

The area of the base point in → **8** shows that the gap between the prefabricated concrete part and the base plate is closed with flexible insulation and a sealing layer on the outside. These two building elements can be subject to stress and can possibly fail due to movements of the façade.

The different layers must be particularly carefully planned around openings. Since the layers are separate they must be joined to avoid direct air flow through the joints. In addition, the different thermal expansion coefficients of the materials used can lead to joint fatigue and thus, in the long term, to air leakage → **15+16**.

16

Rear-ventilated façade
The wall made of prefabricated concrete components requires airtight sealing on the inside. The insulation and the veneer wall do not contribute to airtight sealing.

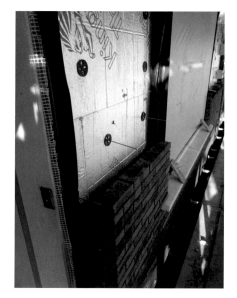

15

Window connection in a rear-ventilated façade
Window connection detail. The sealing also serves to drain water from the air layer.

NOISE PROTECTION

Noise protection in a massive wall construction

Due to the massive building materials, the monolithic building method generally features good noise protection characteristics. In an acoustic sense, its single-shell construction vibrates as a whole. In principle, massive buildings consist of single-shell concrete or brick walls. Deviations of the sound protection characteristics derive from the different densities of the building materials. As shown in → **13**, aerated concrete bricks were chosen in this example. The pores in the material ensure good insulation properties; however, its relatively low density causes lower sound protection properties. The principle of 'the heavier, the better' applies. Generally, the sound protection of the overall building depends on the building element with the lowest sound reduction index, or sound reduction performance. Therefore, the sound reduction index of the windows or the roller shutter casings determine the overall sound protection performance. The windows must be airtight in order to achieve the desired sound reduction index.

In the entrance area of the single-family home → **4**, the single-shell wall construction is clearly visible. The impact sound-insulating of the floating screed of the indoor floor can be seen below the temporary boarding of the entry door. Since the screed floats and does not touch the walls, sound bridges are avoided, and impact sound cannot dissipate from one room to another.

Noise protection in a wall construction with thermal insulation composite system

A classic thermal insulation composite system consists of two layers (excluding the plaster layer) and is therefore considered a multi-layer wall construction. Contrary to the rear-ventilated wall constructions, in terms of acoustics, this construction type features a bending-resistant, firm composite; i.e. with small distances between the layers. The function principle of the soundproofing follows the mass-spring principle, whereby the insulation material represents the 'spring'. This example used an almost fully closed porous insulation material (XPS) with high dynamic rigidity for which no noteworthy improvement of sound reduction (as compared to a single-shell wall) can be expected. This means that the dynamic rigidity – the springiness of the insulation layer – determines the sound transmission. With regard to sound protection, soft mineral wool would achieve better results.

The detail view in → **17** shows the glued, bending-resistant connection between the loadbearing layer (reinforced concrete) and the insulation layer (XPS). As described, the structure of heat insulation composite systems can influence the sound reduction index of an exterior wall. Depending on the mounting method – gluing, gluing with dowels as well as dowels and rail fastening – , the sound protection performance of the wall construction can be decreased. The dowels penetrate the insulation layer and are fastened in the loadbearing layer. They therefore create local thermal and sound bridges.

Penetrations of the entire wall cross-section, for example for technical building devices such as exterior wall sockets or water connections, are critical aspects of sound protection. The same is true for large apertures, for example for exhaust-air systems. Sound protection is impossible in these areas.

17

Detail view of wall construction with thermal insulation composite system
The thermal insulation composite system of the multi-family home is glued to the loadbearing reinforced concrete wall. The adhesive is visible at the joints.

Noise protection in a rear-ventilated wall construction

The rear-ventilated wall construction is a multi-shell construction type, consisting of at least two building elements with a gap between them. The exterior weatherproof layer, here clinker, is separated from the insulation as well as the loadbearing layer by a rear-ventilation zone. This wall setup improves the soundproofing properties according to the mass-spring principle. The air layer in the gap between the two vibrating leaves acts as a spring. The determining factors for improving the sound-insulating are the material of the exterior shell as well as the execution of the ventilation gaps.

The clinker used in → 18 exhibits good soundproofing properties due to its relatively high density. In combination with the reinforced concrete loadbearing layer, the soundproofing properties are improved further due to the different resonance frequencies. The point connections of the exterior shell with the loadbearing layer are accomplished with rustproof wall ties (alternatively bracing systems). These wall ties locally penetrate the insulation layer and are firmly connected with the loadbearing layer. However, these necessary point penetrations (approximately five wire-wound ties per m²) also cause local sound bridges that limit good sound protection.

The lower sound reduction index of individual building elements such as windows and doors influences the entire sound protection. Since the share of window areas and the entry door of the residential house compared to the exterior wall area is relatively large, and the overall sound protection performance is determined by the weakest link, the entry door is of particular importance. The detail view → 19 shows that the interior floor is structurally decoupled from the exterior wall construction to avoid that solid-borne sound is transmitted to adjacent building elements.

18

Plinth area of a rear-ventilated exterior wall construction
In the single-family home, the plinth area was executed with water-resistant insulation in the splash water zone. The point connections between the veneer wall and the loadbearing layer are accomplished with rustproof wall ties.

19

Door area of a rear-ventilated exterior wall construction
Wall construction of the single-family rowhouse before installing the door; floor with underfloor heating to the right.

8 Building Physics and Materials

The materials used for and in buildings play an important role in attuning and adjusting the indoor climate according to the needs of the occupants. The most commonly used materials are inorganic mineral materials such as concrete, clay bricks, gypsum or building bricks. But organic materials like timber, plastics or insulation material on polymer basis, or metals such as steel, iron or aluminium also belong to the common building material portfolio. All of these materials behave very differently with regard to mechanical as well as building physics aspects. Thus, choosing a specific material can be a beneficial means to achieve the desired indoor climate. Not everyone is fully aware of what kind of an impact sun, rain, wind as well as sound or light have on the materials used in and on buildings. It therefore makes sense to explain and understand these climatic boundary conditions and their physical influences in more detail. The overview → **1** shows and evaluates specific aspects of commonly used building materials.

Building physics describes how and why molecules within a building material are excited by external conditions. The excitement is caused by various environmental conditions such as solar radiation, rain, sound or wind, amongst others. Materials respond dynamically to these influences or even change their properties. These reactions can influence the indoor climate of buildings and therefore our sense of comfort. Accordingly, knowledge of the relationship between material behaviour and ambient climate is of major importance. The approach presented in this chapter, which states that material properties are in direct interdependency with the effects of building physics, serves to better understand the described dependencies and to offer a holistic view. New materials are constantly developed and brought to market in order to comply with the different and sometimes conflictive demands already discussed. Special emphasis should be given to ecologically sustainable materials that are proven to fulfil the building physics requirements in daily practice.

Influence / Material	Heat	Moisture	Sound	Light	Air
Concrete	+	++	++	−	+
Brick	+	−−	−	++	+
Steel	−−	+	−−	++	++
Glass	−−	++	−	++	++
Timber	++	−−	−	+	−

1

Overview of commonly used materials and their building physics performances
It becomes obvious that one single material cannot optimally fulfil all requirements.

CONCRETE

Concrete as the most commonly used building material is a mineral material that consists of cement, aggregate (i.e. gravel or sand) and water. An indefinite number of different types of concrete can be made from these raw ingredients, each of which exhibits different mechanical and building physics properties. Concrete's general performance with regard to the building physics factors heat, moisture, sound, light and air will be evaluated in the following → **2+3**.

Concrete and thermal energy

There are two significant factors that influence the heat-related behaviour of concrete; namely heat conduction and heat storage capacity. Both of these properties play an important role for buildings in extreme climate regions. The thermal conductivity of concrete is comparably high, which is why heat loss through a concrete wall is also relatively high. On the other hand, concrete exhibits a very large thermal storage capacity; therefore, a lot of thermal energy can be stored in a concrete wall before heat begins flowing toward the outside. This aspect is particularly exploited in warm countries where thick concrete walls do not serve a structural but rather a building physics purpose in order to protect the interior from external solar radiation. Solar heat is stored in the concrete walls during daytime, and in the evening or at night, when temperatures drop, it is returned to the surroundings.

Concrete and moisture

The absorption and desorption capacity of concrete, i.e. the capability to take on and release moisture, together with the capacity to transport moisture or other liquids through the porous structure are important factors in building physics. Both of these properties are determined by the inner porous structure of concrete, whereby the total volume of pores as well as the connectivity of the pores play an important role. Per definition concretes with high water-cement values have a high water content, which, after curing, forms the pores. With common types of concrete, these pore spaces and therefore the capillary pores are often connected, creating an internal network. This network enables moisture transportation through a wall construction from the outside to the inside or vice versa. These processes are very important in terms of a moisture balance because these paths offer a means for moisture exchange with the surrounding space.

Concrete and acoustics

Sound is a physical phenomenon that propagates in the air or in the material itself via waves, thereby carrying a certain amount of energy. These waves can be caused by people, machines, automobiles or other ambient influences, and can therefore excite walls or other building elements into vibration. The properties of the materials that walls, floors or ceilings of a room are made of also determine implicitly how the waves behave upon coming into contact with a building element. Hereby, the mass and the elasticity of a material are important factors. With regard to airborne sound, and due to its relatively high raw density, concrete features good soundproofing properties compared to other building materials. The waves are almost completely reflected, hardly exciting the concrete at all, which means that the sound energy is not transmitted through the wall. Impact or solid-borne sound is a different matter; here, the waves are transmitted directly through the concrete or other materials with a similarly high raw density. This means that sound is spread and transmitted to adjacent rooms. To avoid this, measures must be employed that interrupt the sound waves. Such measures include installing insulation beneath floating screed, decoupling the floor construction of adjacent rooms and including edge insulation strips between screed and wall.

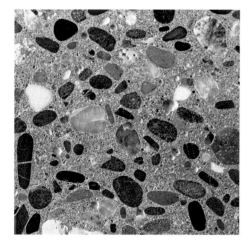

2

Section through a concrete body
The components gravel and cement stone are clearly discernible after a saw cut through a concrete body.

Concrete and light

Depending on the colour of a material, light, i.e. light waves, is transmitted, absorbed or reflected. In the case of grey or dark grey concrete, light is generally reflected and/or absorbed. As described before, concrete exhibits a very high heat storage capacity, causing it to absorb the thermal energy of light or solar radiation. Therefore, there is no transmission of light. The colour of concrete can be altered with the help of different types of cement, which in turn means that the influence of light, i.e. the degree of reflection or absorption, can be adjusted to specific conditions.

Concrete and air

The air quality inside a building should not be influenced by the choice of material. Different materials can play a significant role, depending on their use or function in the building. Concrete has the advantage that it features a very dense structure and therefore cannot store air and is odourless. And concrete surfaces can be easily coated, if so desired. When considering air quality inside buildings, it can be assumed that no air exchange takes place with the surroundings through a concrete surface.

3

Radio Kootwijk, Building A, Apeldoorn, Julius Luthmann, 1918
The aesthetic effect of this Art Deco building is enhanced by the grey concrete.

BRICK

Traditional bricks are made of clay that is fired in a kiln. Alternatively, bricks can be made of calcareous lime. In both cases the result is a solid body with an open porous structure on the inside, just like concrete. The resulting properties mainly depend on the firing temperature. The raw density of a brick can vary between $1400\,kg/m^3$ and $1800\,kg/m^3$ → **4+5**.

Brick and thermal energy

Since the raw density of a brick is significantly lower than that of concrete, brick's thermal conductivity and heat storage capacity also differ significantly from those of concrete. The raw density of brick is lower because brick has more pores and therefore contains more air. This also means that the thermal conductivity of dry bricks is lower than that of concrete. With moist bricks, the absorbed water plays an important role and therefore implicitly determines its thermal conductivity, which increases. The heat storage capacity of brick is lower than that of concrete. The material's open porous structure results in less mass, which in turn means that heat cannot be stored for a longer period of time.

Brick and moisture

The described open porous structure of brick allows for moisture to easily penetrate the pore space and accumulate there. Generally speaking, the pores within a brick are connected with each other and thus form a network. Therefore, water can easily move inside a brick, which means that in a masonry wall the capillary action can cause water to shift vertically. Often, countermeasures are taken to inhibit the rising of moisture inside brickwork. These measures typically include horizontal or vertical barriers, or trass frames. A trass frame is a portion of a brick wall five to six brick courses below and above the ground. It is made of hard natural stone or specially burnt bricks to prevent moisture from rising upward inside the wall.

4

Masonry
Masonry or brickwork consists of bricks and joints.
Different joint designs create visual variations.

5

Façade of an Amsterdam School residential building, Amsterdam, Hendrik Wijdeveld, 1917–1921
The detail shows typical decorative brickwork.

Brick and acoustics

Since brick has a relatively low mass, sound waves can relatively easily propagate through brick walls. A brick wall is lighter than a concrete wall and therefore poses less resistance against reflecting and/or absorbing air waves. In terms of solid-borne or impact sound, a brick wall can be more effective because the related sound waves cannot propagate as easily through an open porous medium. The open porous structure can also cause waves in a brick wall to be absorbed, resulting in a sound-insulating effect.

Brick and light

Bricks are manufactured in different colours and types. With these variations it is possible to influence a brick wall's degree of absorption and/or reflection. The different colours determine how much light energy is reflected and how much can be stored in the wall. Both properties have an immediate effect on the building physics behaviour of a building element. The reflection of a brick wall also determines the amount of light that can enter a room → **6**.

Brick and air

A mineral material such as brick is an inert material that does not influence the air quality of a room. The open porous structure makes it possible that moisture can easily be absorbed from and dissipated to the indoor climate. This can have a positive effect on the indoor climate because high humidity levels can be decreased through short-term absorption and reintroduced into the room from the bricks to the indoor air over time.

6

Castle Huis Bergh, 's-Heerenberg, dating back to the 13th century
Façade design with brickwork.

STEEL

Steel is a frequently used material with a very high raw density of 7850 kg/m³. It does not contain pores or pore structures, and its building physics properties therefore differ significantly from mineral materials → **7**.

Steel and thermal energy

Since steel has a very high thermal conductivity, it can easily warm up. And due to its high raw density, it can also store large amounts of thermal energy. In general, it is considered as disadvantageous that the stored amount of heat can, in turn, dissipate very quickly, too, which means that the stored energy cannot be used as heat storage. But the material's high thermal conductivity can be employed advantageously when large amounts of heat need to be dissipated quickly.

Steel and moisture

The crystalline structure of steel is so dense that the material is entirely watertight and does not allow water inclusion or storage. Moisture transmission through capillary action is not possible either. Therefore, steel can also be used for water or moisture-proofing on façades or roofs. Many other application opportunities lie in those fields that require a combination of high thermal capacity and high thermal conductivity in combination with water-tightness as material properties. This is the reason why steel is used for roof cladding or cladding of separating and exterior walls, for example. In these cases, it is important that the walls are water-resistant and equipped with an anti-corrosion coating. In addition, quick heat dissipation must be possible to prevent excessive expansion.

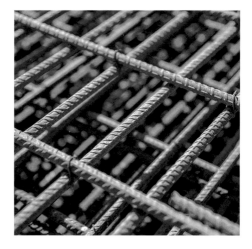

7

Steel
Steel in the form of reinforcement inside concrete is an indispensable material.

8

City of Arts and Sciences, Valencia, Santiago Calatrava and Félix Candela, 1998
Steel used as a loadbearing façade element.

Steel and acoustics

The sound absorption capacity of steel is relatively low due to the high elasticity modulus and a very high raw density, resulting in a very rigid, dense material. Airborne sound waves that strike a steel surface are reflected without loss and returned into the room. In addition, impact sound waves can spread easily and quickly through steel. This means that steel is not very suited as sound absorption material or sound-insulating.

Steel and light

If the surface is polished, steel can almost act like a mirror, and almost all incident light is reflected. However, rust formation has an influence on the share of reflected light; it reduces it. On the other hand, steel can be employed as a reflective element intentionally to reduce the light energy demand required for a room → **8+9**.

Steel and air

Since steel is a very dense, airtight material, it cannot be used as a filter in the sense of building physics. Due to its high density, the building industry also uses steel as an airtight barrier to protect certain areas within a building → **10**.

9

C. R. Crown Hall, Illinois Institute of Technology, Chicago, Ludwig Mies van der Rohe, 1956
Steel and glass façade.

10

Façade detail, C. R. Crown Hall
Posts and beams made of steel as a design element.

GLASS

The mineral material glass is light-transmissive, very brittle, has a dense structure and a raw density of approximately 2500 kg/m³. Glass, such as window glass, for example, is an amorphous solid that mainly consists of pure siliceous sand. In terms of building physics, glass can be employed with various intentions → **11**.

Glass and thermal energy

In the field of heat protection, glass plays an important role. Since it is light-transmissive, solar radiation, i.e. solar heat, can reach the inside of a building through the glass and illuminate and thereby heat interior surfaces. Important factors are energy transmittance, the number of glass layers (single, double or triple glazing), the entrance angle and possible sun protection measures. In this case it is important that the materials chosen inside the rooms have a high storage capacity in order to prevent excessive temperatures and overheating during the hot summer months. Different types of glass or glass coatings can limit the intensity of incident heat or, if so desired, facilitate it → **12+13**.

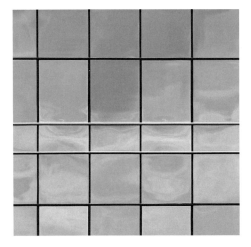

11

Glass façade
In the building industry, this indispensable material is an essential part of any façade.

12

Office building Duoc Antonio Varas, Santiago de Chile, Juan Sabbagh Pisano, 2008
Reflective glass elements award the façade lightness and modernity.

Glass and moisture

The moisture-related properties of a glass pane are primarily defined by a watertight installation because the high density of glass does not permit any water absorption or water transmittance through the material itself. Single-pane glass windows pose the risk of water condensation on the glass pane, which can cool down significantly during winter. Due to their lower thermal conductivity, double or triple glazing exhibits higher surface temperatures, and therefore, a significantly smaller risk of water condensation.

Glass and acoustics

Since glass has a hard surface structure, incident sound waves are reflected on the surface without losing sound energy. The elasticity modulus of glass is similar to that of granite, for example. Therefore, it is to be expected that in a room with a large share of window area there will be significant reflection of the sound waves. The reflections lead to strong reverberant sounds, which has a negative effect on the understandability during conversations and therefore the sense of comfort. In these cases, special absorptive surfaces are needed that can absorb the sound waves and thus reduce the reverberation period.

Glass and light

One of glass' most important properties is its crystalline structure and the resulting transparency. This makes glass to be a unique material for which there are no alternatives. For the human being, transparency largely defines the type of comfort we experience indoors. Hereby, light plays a dominant role, generally being the primary aspect that enables us to live inside a building. In addition, the application of glass coatings or coloured glass can influence the human experience of a room. This means that next to its function in the building, glass also has a dimension that can strongly influence the human sense of comfort.

Glass and air

Since glass has a very dense crystalline structure, no pores, and is not air-permeable, it can only be used for airtight building elements. Additionally, glass itself is odourless and therefore does not require special post-processing. Considering the high density of glass, any use of larger glass areas must be accompanied by considerations on how to ventilate the indoor space.

13

Detail of the office building
Duoc Antonio Varas, Santiago de Chile
The entire façade area consists of glass.

WOOD

The organic material wood is a naturally grown material with many different properties that mechanically and in terms of building physics depend on the orientation (anisotropic), the origin and the type of the wood. Each sort has its own porosity, its own anisotropic property and its individual hygrothermic behaviour. Therefore, the properties of wood are species-specific, but vary within one species depending on the origin of a specific tree. The most common types of wood in the building industry are relatively light and feature raw densities of between 500 kg/m³ and 700 kg/m³. Hardwood can have raw densities of up to 1000 kg/m³. However, the raw density fluctuates significantly depending on the moisture content of the wood because the water in the pores influences the building physics and mechanical properties → **14+15**.

Wood and thermal energy

Wood features very good thermal conductivity and heat storage capacity. Its high thermal capacity makes it suitable for applications in buildings and/or flats that require heat protection in summer. Since many types of wood have very low raw densities (lighter than water), the overall storage capacity of traditional building timber is much lower than that of concrete. The raw density of concrete is twice to three times that of wood. The low thermal conductivity properties make wood a relatively good insulation material. For residential buildings these are beneficial properties, for timber walls have good insulation properties and can store the accumulated heat for a long period of time.

14

Cross-section of a timber log
The image shows cracks resulting from drying.

15

Trees before processing
The location of a tree and the climatic conditions of the location determine the quality of the wood.

Wood and moisture

Wood has an organic structure and is bio-degradable; it can easily decay when infested by wood-destructing insects or fungi. The most important environmental influence that determines the intensity of the process of decay is air humidity or the wood moisture balance that occurs in the wood due to the ambient air humidity. Therefore, it is paramount that wood is well protected or treated against ambient influences. With regard to building physics, water condensation at or in timber constructions must therefore be prevented; usually this is achieved with sufficient ventilation. Only then can timber maintain its construction-related properties. Timber constructions always require a careful moisture balance → **16+17**.

Wood and acoustics

Since wood has a relatively low raw density and a low elasticity modulus, it is less suited as sound protection material. Specifically in the case of airborne soundproofing, whereby mass plays an important role, wood has little to offer to counteract sound waves. In the case of impact sound, wood fares a little better because its porous structure lets it absorb or internally dissipate impact sound waves. Most commonly, wood is used in the form of sound-insulating panels because it is easy to process. Examples are wave dispersion elements or flexible wall elements to absorb sound waves.

Wood and light

In combination with light, wood's beautiful outer structure offers architects many possibilities for unique interior design. Therefore, the material is often used in indoor spaces in the form of wood panelling or wood floors.

Wood and air

Fresh wood has a strong characteristic odour. Sometimes this is desirable but often the wood is post-processed to achieve a neutral odour and to prevent the material taking on other unwanted smells.

16

Residential building covered with wood shingles
The shingles protect the loadbearing construction against weather conditions.

17

Detail of the wooden façade
Vertically and horizontally overlapping shingles ensure protection against driving rain.

Engineered wood products

In building practice, mostly engineered wood products are used because they allow for almost any geometry and dimensioning of wooden building elements. Engineered wood products consist of several wood elements glued together, such as strands, veneer, planks or battens. Classic examples of engineered wood products are glue-laminated timber (glulam) → **18**, laminated veneer lumber (LVL) → **19** and laminated strand lumber (LSL) → **20**. Glue-laminated timber is made by gluing wood pieces such as battens or boards into long wood elements. The adhesion in longitudinal and cross-direction allows for elements of various length and cross-section geometry. Laminated veneer lumber consists of glued wood veneers whose fibres are all oriented in the same direction. The advantage over glue-laminated lumber is that planar building elements can be made as well, such as loadbearing wall and ceiling elements, for example. Laminated strand lumber consists of relatively large glued wood strands. The product is typically applied in the form of laminar building elements, amongst which are wall and ceiling panels. Since the strands are positioned in a homogenous orientation, the resulting panels offer only one-directional loadbearing capability. The main advantage of engineered wood products over solid wood is its greater form stability. The gluing and the orientation of the fibres of wood products counteract the deformation behaviour that is typical for solid wood, e.g. swelling and contracting. This increases the quality and loadbearing capacity of the construction.

20

Laminated strand lumber (LSL)
Gluing together equally orientated strands makes linear and planar building elements.

18

Glue-laminated timber (glulam)
Wood pieces glued together in vertical and horizontal direction can be used for supports, beams and other building elements that are subjected to bending loads.

19

Laminated veneer lumber (LVL)
Single wood veneers are glued together with consistent fibre orientation.

OTHER ECOLOGICAL BUILDING MATERIALS

Latest developments in the field of building materials focus on natural materials such as clay, straw and various types of fibres, e.g. stemming from bamboo or sisal plants. The advantage of these materials over others is that their production does not require great energy expenditure. They can be used in their original state, as they occur in nature. Natural materials are often used in combination with conventional materials. These so-called composite materials make it possible that specific properties such as insulation capacity, heat flow and/or heat storage capacity can be varied across the composite's cross-section. It makes sense to build up integrated sandwich panels made from different materials in a way that the layers maintain their building physics properties.

A stone layer with concrete insertion and a clay layer, for example, together form an ecological concrete wall element with very good insulation and energy storage capacities → **21+22**. In addition, this layered material's relatively high specific mass also gives it good sound-absorbing properties. The use of such innovative material concepts allows for environmentally friendly and energy-efficient building methods and minimal energy usage during the building's life span. The specific performance capabilities of these composite materials must be carefully considered before practical application.

21

Sandwich building elements made of clay and concrete
These building elements form a sustainable system to construct and insulate the building envelope.

22

Building elements made of rammed clay
Recyclability also plays an important role when choosing suitable building materials.

9 Building Physics and the Building Envelope

DEMANDS ON THE BUILDING ENVELOPE

The building envelope constitutes a climate barrier between the interior and the exterior and allows us to feel comfortable in a building even under uncomfortable weather conditions. It forms the border between the preferably constant temperature and humidity level inside and fluctuating atmospheric conditions outside. Consequently, the building envelope is constantly subjected to the loads from different energy flows trying to balance each other out. Therefore, the materials and the structure of the building envelope must fulfil the building physics requirements of heat, moisture, airtightness, sound and light.

Heat insulation

In terms of heat insulation in winter, the building envelope must feature sufficient insulating properties, which means that either the entire construction – e.g. a massive wall construction – must be well-insulated, or that the individual layers, e.g. in case of a rear-ventilated façade, take on this function.

Measures of heat protection serve to prevent overheating through solar radiation during summer. This mainly concerns transparent construction elements that should be equipped with sun protection systems such as louvres or coatings, for example. Opaque construction elements automatically fulfil these requirements with the insulation properties they feature for winter. In both cases, construction elements with highly effective heat storage capacity contribute to the indoor protection against exterior conditions.

Moisture proofing

Wall and façade constructions must be able to shield against rain or even driving rain as well as manage the different humidity levels of the inside and the outside. The outer layer usually ensures protection against rain, whereby, depending on the construction, additional layers can be included to drain water, even within the construction. In terms of building construction, a differentiation is made between rain, driving rain (with an impact angle of up to 90 degrees depending on wind conditions) and splash water (which is reflected upward upon hitting hard surfaces).

Next to rain, the second important aspect is humidity, meaning the water bound in the air, and its effect on the construction. It can wet the construction either due to pressure difference or rain. The same happens when temperatures change, resulting in different degrees of water absorbance of the air. Thus, the building envelope must either be able to prevent humidity from entering the construction or absorb the water and drain it toward the outside via appropriate systems.

Airtightness

What is true for heat and moisture is also valid for airtightness; the interior and the exterior of a building must be strictly separated. In this case, the sealing of the building envelope serves to prevent draught in the interior spaces. Draught can result from unwanted leakages due to a combination of air movement and air temperature, but also from intentional ventilating to ensure hygienic and comfortable conditions. But sealing the building envelope is also important from an energetic point of view, since it prevents energy losses caused by exhausting warm air.

It is at least as important to keep room air humidity away from the construction in order to prevent moisture, as explained in Chapter 3, 'Moisture'. This requires a dependable sealing between the indoor space and the building envelope. Careful planning and execution is necessary to prevent leakages.

The more airtight a building is, the more important is proper ventilation. Natural ventilation can be achieved through windows. Hereby, it is not so much the construction element itself that warrants airtightness, but rather the joints, for example, between window and massive wall. Besides the construction element, these details must be planned to be completely airtight, which is especially true for movable elements.

Acoustics

A building envelope also serves as sound protection by damping airborne sound so that street noise, for example, cannot easily penetrate the interior space. This can either be accomplished with mass – meaning heavy constructions – that does not vibrate easily and therefore damps sound impulses. Or a spring-mass principle can be employed: here, the individual layers of the construction – a rear-ventilated wall construction, for example – act differently to different sound impulses. This delays or reduces the vibrational behaviour and therefore also dampens sound.

The building envelope equally influences the room acoustics – reverberation effects occur depending on how well the surfaces reflect the sound to the interior. However, usually the surface area of the façade-facing wall is proportionally smaller than that of the other walls and ceiling surfaces in a room and, thus, not as critical. A second aspect to consider is sound transport by sound wave propagation within construction elements.

Light

Comfortable lighting of an indoor space can only be accomplished with sufficient transparent areas in the building envelope. The yield of natural daylight depends on the size and the location/arrangement of the apertures. These decisions also impact the energy demand for artificial light. Geographic orientation determines the potential solar gain, an important aspect in terms of heat input (see Chapter 2, 'Thermal Energy') as well as illumination levels. Depending on the intensity, the illumination level can be a positive factor if it provides sufficient lighting, but can also cause glare, a negative aspect that needs to be dealt with.

The influx of daylighting also influences our visual comfort, meaning a connection from the inside to the outside. Since light is a quickly changing parameter, certainly throughout the course of a day, it should be ensured that transparent areas of the façade can be adapted to the demands of the users by installing sun protection and glare protection systems.

1

Massive wall
This natural stone masonry forms a massive loadbearing wall.

2

Shingle façade
The shingle cover on a skeleton construction acts as protection against rain.

Contradictions in the combinations of different demands

In terms of the demands in the building envelope, the above described aspects heat, moisture, airtightness, sound and light require very different technical solutions:

Insulation is best accomplished with very light constructions with small pores or thin layers to prevent air change (convection). This is contradicted by the requirements of good sound-insulating as well as of the exploitation of thermal mass since such measures require heavy constructions to achieve sufficient storage mass. A similar contradiction occurs when conceptualising a building envelope with sufficient sun protection: shading devices or sun protection coatings conflict with the desire for maximum yield of daylight.

4

Metal frame construction
North American metal frame façade during construction.

3

Timber frame construction
North American timber construction (balloon framing) during construction.

5

Rear-ventilated façade
This façade consists of a layered system combining a rain protection layer and an insulating/loadbearing structure.

Against the background of structural joints in the building envelope, the problem of heat exchange between the inside and the outside must also be discussed: connection elements are needed to transfer structural loads. For the sake of loadbearing capacity they need to have more mass, which at the same time increases their heat conductivity, with the adverse result of thermal bridges. They can be minimised by layering and load concentration but cannot be completely avoided.

Another construction-related issue is the necessity of butt joints between construction elements. Butt joints are always weak areas in terms of rain and airtightness. They should be avoided as much as possible, which, however, requires compromises in the case of prefabricated construction elements: to comply with transport requirements they are usually limited in size and must be joined on site. Butt joints are also unavoidable at the transitions of construction elements, for example between massive wall and window. It can be helpful to try and reduce the number of butt joints by solving the details with technically known and established construction principles. A building envelope can be as homogenous as possible, but it will always show such problematic areas; they cannot be fully avoided. A building envelope must meet these contradicting requirements – whereby all aspects must be addressed optimally in order to create an energy-efficient building → **3–5**.

FAÇADE CONSTRUCTION TYPES

Three principal systems can be employed to solve the different requirements posed on a façade: massive construction, which integrates all requirements; layered construction, in which the individual requirements are solved with individual layers; and skeleton or frame constructions, in which the loadbearing function is separated from the space-enclosing function.

The advantage of massive façade constructions is their simplicity → **6+7**. A construction that is essentially made of a single material can be produced rather easily because it does not require elaborate connections between different layers. Later modifications are rarely a problem. Massive constructions contribute to the structural integrity of the overall building. However, it is difficult to optimise such constructions with regard to individual requirements, since – as described – the requirements often contradict each other and can rarely be fully met by the material properties only. And massive construction cannot be used for all functions of a building: doors, windows and other construction elements must be integrated into the building envelope, always requiring penetration.

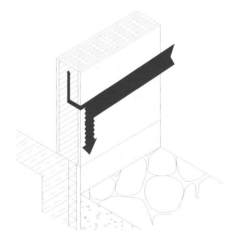

7

Moisture transition massive wall
When rain hits the exterior of a massive wall, part of the water drains off in fluid state, another part penetrates and wets the material and can escape to the interior.

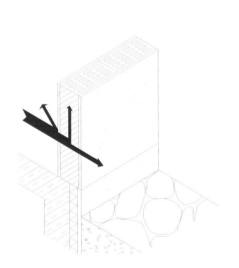

6

Heat transition massive wall
When heat acts on a massive wall, part of it is reflected and another part is stored in the wall. But part of the thermal energy is lost through the wall.

Building envelopes in the form of a layered construction – rearventilated façades, for example – on the other hand are well suited to fulfil the different requirements related to heat, moisture, airtightness, sound and light with individual layers. The combination allows to optimise individual layers in terms of their performance without restricting the function of the overall construction. A disadvantage is the complexity of the construction, in terms of assembly as well as later, when the building envelope requires modification and various layers must be adapted.

Of those three types, skeleton constructions are the most differentiated construction types: the loadbearing function is separated from the space-enclosing function by setting up a support framework, onto which the space-enclosing panels or construction elements are mounted. These fulfil the different demands on the building envelope, and thereby increase the efficiency of the entire construction: it becomes more slender and thus more efficient, glass panes are easy to add to optimise transparency.

Massive wall construction

Massive walls are characterised by simple connections and their potential loadbearing capacity → **8+10**. Furthermore, a massive wall exhibits a certain heat-insulating property since it prevents direct radiation and convection. Thermal energy, on the other hand, can be transferred due to the good thermal conductance of the mass. If this is to be prevented, the massive construction needs to be made lighter so that less mass provides less conductance. This is typically accomplished with cavities in the construction elements, in the form of chambers (e.g. hollow bricks → **9**) or cavities in the original material (e.g. aerated concrete). In general, massive constructions can store heat well. But the storage capacity is reduced the lighter the construction is.

9

Chambers in hollow bricks
Air chambers inside hollow bricks reduce the thermal conductivity of the bricks and therefore improve their insulation properties.

8

Plinth detail with recess in a massive wall
An additional insulation layer can be mounted in the recess in the lower part to allow for continuous thermal insulation.

10

Sealing a plinth
To protect it from splash water, the plinth area is sealed with bituminous sheeting.

Massive walls can be sealed against incoming moisture if the construction is watertight, for example with waterproof concrete or plaster layers, or the material intentionally absorbs the moisture, as is the case with bricks, for example. Hereby it is important that the material is not damaged by taking on water and that the water can dry off. This requires a detailed examination of moisture development in construction elements across the different seasons of the year to prevent permanent wetting. Areas that are particularly impacted, by groundwater or splash water for example, require additional sealing.

With massive walls, airtightness is generally unproblematic; it is guaranteed by the dimension and does not require specific consideration. The same is true for airborne sound protection because it is difficult to excite massive constructions into vibration. Only impact sound, which is transmitted by the material, can be problematic; however, it does not concern so much the separation of the outside and the inside but rather sound transmission within the building. Windows and door openings fulfil the demands in respect to light in most cases.

Layered façade construction

With layered constructions, or rear-ventilated façades, the loadbearing layer is separated from the insulating layer. In addition, an air layer and a rain-repellent layer are placed before the insulating layer → **11+12**. Since the functions loadbearing and insulation are separated, the insulation layer can be implemented rather easily. The additional air layer and the rain-repellent layer protect the insulation against exterior influences such as water, solar radiation and mechanical stress. Another advantage is that the inner construction can be massive and thus better store thermal energy. This makes the building thermally inert, and thereby creates a comfortable indoor climate.

One disadvantage of this construction is its complexity resulting from the layered structure. The plinth detail shows that besides the loadbearing function from the inner construction to the foundation, all other functional layers such as insulation, air gap and rainproofing must be constructed as separate elements, and each needs to transfer its loads individually. Similar constructive solutions are needed where construction elements, such as windows for example, need to be joined.

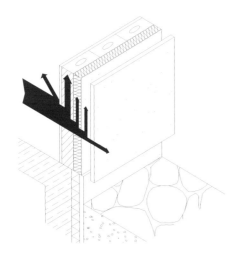

11

Heat transition through rear-ventilated wall
The heat from the indoor room is partially reflected and partially stored in the massive and the insulating layer. Small shares penetrate the wall and are absorbed in the air gap and the waterproofing layer.

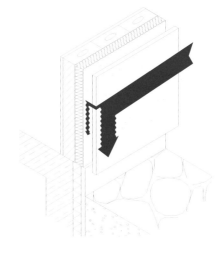

12

Moisture transition through rear-ventilated wall
Rain on exterior rainproofing layer: the largest share runs off immediately. In case of penetration (defects), moisture is systematically drained inside the wall system.

In terms of moisture-proofing, rear-ventilated façades pose the advantage that the exterior rainproof layer repels rain as well as driving rain. If water does penetrate this layer, it is systematically drained away in the air layer. Depending on the interior (loadbearing) wall construction, vapour pressure is kept from the inside either by the material itself or by a vapour-proof foil.

Airtightness is ensured by the massive inner layer, or by a vapour-tight foil on the inner layer. In terms of noise protection, the different layers act like a mass-spring system. However, this is rather negligable since the massive inner layer provides the largest part of the noise-protecting function due to its low vibrations. Similar to massive constructions, the requirements of lighting can be easily handled with windows and doors → **13–15**.

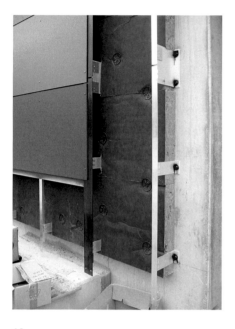

13

Layered structure of rear-ventilated façade
The layering makes it necessary to constructively connect the individual layers of the façade.

14

Rear-ventilated sheet metal façade
Typical solution for the plinth detail of a rear-ventilated façade. The upper area shows the individual layers; the lower area shows a massive construction with core insulation.

15

Rear-ventilated façade
The individual layers for loadbearing (concrete), insulation, airtightness and waterproofing are clearly visible. The plinth area contains a water-resistant core insulation.

Skeleton construction

Skeleton constructions are usually executed as timber constructions or post-and-beam systems. As the term implies, the loads of the building are transferred by a skeleton or frame, while sealing and insulating are accommodated in the panels that are mounted onto the loadbearing system. Transparency, i.e. allowing light transmission into the building, is provided by glass panels. Hereby, it is necessary to design a second glass layer in order to interrupt heat conduction. It has been shown that a gap of around 15 mm between the glass panes causes the convection in this area to cease, and this reduces the potential of heat conduction. In order to further improve the insulation property, a third pane creating another gap can be added → **16+18**.

Besides partial and angle-dependent reflection, a restricted spectrum of solar radiation still penetrates the glass panes. It heats up the glass pane as well as the indoor space. In autumn, winter and spring this might be desirable, but it can lead to overheating in summer. Overheating can be prevented with exterior shading or metallic, reflective coatings on the glass. However, these measures have an immediate effect on the light permeability of the construction, which must be controlled accordingly → **17**.

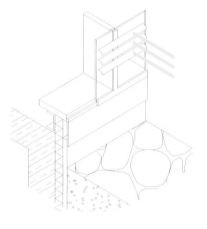

17

Shading of the glazing
In order to reduce incident light, light-reflecting sun protection systems are installed in front of the glass layer.

16

Heat transition through post-and-beam structure
Heat is reflected by the insulating glass pane, partially penetrates the glazing and is transported to the interior.

18

Rain water drainage on a post-and-beam façade
For the most part, rain is drained off on the exterior glass panes and the exterior profiles. If it does penetrate the construction, it is drained off within the wall system.

With post-and-beam façades, water is drained off right on the outside surface. In case of leakage, a second draining layer within the system comes into play that collects incoming water and drains it to the outside at the bottom of the construction. The impermeability of the system largely depends on the chosen joint profiles of the construction and the way the nodes are executed. Typically, the construction projects out from the underlying foundation to allow for drainage. This also prevents driving rain from coming into contact with the foundation.

The required airtightness is achieved with profiled joints in the construction. Due to its low mass, a post-and-beam structure can provide less noise protection than the other types of construction. Even though the mass-spring principle applies, noise remains the neuralgic spot of skeleton constructions → **19–21**.

20

Example of a plinth construction in semi ready state
Post-and-beam façade and the sealing below it. Insulation and exterior protective layer are installed later.

19

Bottom view of a skeleton façade
Detailed view of a not-yet-sealed plinth area of a post-and-beam structure. Other details shown are glazing support, glazing and the prepared sealing layer of the system.

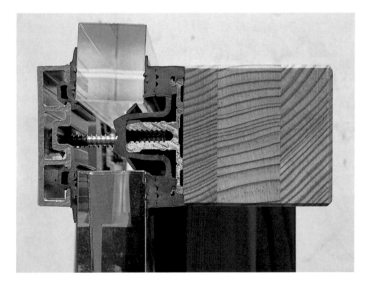

21

Cross-section through the post of a timber-aluminium façade
The outer clamping strip seals the façade against rain; drainage takes place in the gap if water does penetrate the construction. The sealing profiles mounted in the inside keep off diffusing moisture.

FUTURE POTENTIAL

As proven and tested as the individual construction variants and methods are, as continuous is the optimisation of materials and constructions. The focus lies on simpler assembly, improved functionality and lower cost. But research and development are also seeking to improve adaptability and further optimise the insulating properties.

Future potential is also offered by functionally adaptable constructions: a building envelope might be able to not only adapt the existing functions lighting and ventilation, but also react to thermal and acoustic influences in an adaptive manner. A dynamic insulation system that could be activated or reduced depending on the time of day or time of year, offers the opportunity of actively controlling the heat and moisture balance, be it by means of mechanical constructions or integrated in the materials.

Another step could be the energetic activation of the building envelope. Whereas building-integrated photovoltaics (BIPV) is still in its early days, solar heating systems are already established. But these fields still offer potential as well – less in a technical but rather in a functional sense. A related approach to that of solar heating systems is the integration of water pipes (capillary matting) in opaque construction elements to transfer solar energy into heat, and then to store it or use it inside the building. This principle can also be used for cooling.

In the future, the energy needed to produce a construction element will become more critical. Optimised constructions reduce the energy consumption for use so much that the production of construction elements or constructions is so high that it equals the energy for building use for 20 to 30 years. This poses the question whether a construction makes sense if it is designed for a shorter life cycle. As a consequence, constructions made for short-term use will be light, and buildings made for long-term use heavy. The possibility of disassembling a construction and separating materials plays an important role since mono-materials can be recycled better than composites, for example.

And finally, a very up-to-date topic in the field of urban acoustics should be mentioned because it can be well influenced by the building envelope: especially in densely built-up zones noise pollution in the urban space can be significantly reduced with appropriately controlled sound reflection on the outside of the façade – an aspect that has not yet found consideration in the planning processes.

22

**Research project ETA-Fabrik,
Darmstadt Technical University, 2016**
The ETA-Fabrik pioneers energetically optimised factory buildings:
water pipes integrated in the concrete construction store the heat
of solar incidence, and can transmit them to the inside of the building.
In case of overheating, the process can also be reversed.

Authors

Professor Dr.-Ing. Ulrich Knaack was trained as an architect and worked in private practice in Düsseldorf. Currently, he is professor for Construction and Design at Delft University of Technology as well as professor for Façade Structures at Technical University Darmstadt. Author of the well-known reference books *Konstruktiver Glasbau* and *Konstruktiver Glasbau 2*, co-author of the book series *Imagine*.

Professor Dr.ir. Eddie Koenders was awarded his doctoral degree at Delft University of Technology. Today, he is professor at the chair for Building Materials, Building Chemistry and Building Physics and director of the Institute for Construction and Building Materials at Technical University Darmstadt.

Dipl.-Ing. Elena Alexandrakis is doctoral candidate at the Institute for Construction and Building Materials at Technical University Darmstadt and leader of the accredited testing laboratory 'Innovation & Testing Center' of HOCHTIEF Engineering GmbH, responsible for the fields of material and components testing, fastening technology, façade technology and product development.

M.Sc. David Bewersdorff has completed his civil engineering studies at Technical University Darmstadt with a focus on building physics and building redevelopment. Since then, he has been a building physicist in practice at an engineering office. Within the scope of his PhD studies, he conducts research projects at Technical University Darmstadt.

Dipl.-Ing. Ines Haake was scientific staff member at the Institute for Construction and Building Materials at Technical University Darmstadt and is currently working as a soon-to-be authorized expert in a consultancy for building damages.

M.A. Sascha Hickert studied architecture at University of Applied Sciences OWL, Detmold School of Architecture and Interior Architecture, where he completed his master's degree with distinction in 2013. Since 2014, he has been scientific staff member and doctoral candidate in the field of Façade Structures at the Institute of Structural Mechanics and Design, Department of Civil and Environmental Engineering Sciences at Technical University Darmstadt.

M.Sc. Christoph Mankel studied construction engineering at Technical University Darmstadt with a focus in construction above ground. Since 2015, he has been scientific staff member and doctoral candidate at the Institute for Construction and Building Materials at Technical University Darmstadt. His research focus is on energy storage with phase change materials, and he supervises the master's degree activities in 'Structural Building Physics' and 'Computational Methods for Building Physics and Construction Materials'.

Selected bibliography

Thermal Energy

Wolfgang M. Willems, Kai Schild
Wärmeschutz – Grundlagen –
Berechnung – Bewertung
Second edition. Wiesbaden: Springer Vieweg,
2013

DIN EN ISO 7243:2017-12
Ergonomics of the thermal environment –
Assessment of heat stress using the WBGT
(wet bulb globe temperature) index.
Berlin: Beuth, 2017

DIN EN ISO 7730:2006-05
Ergonomics of the thermal environment –
Analytical determination and interpretation
of thermal comfort using calculation of the
PMV and PPD indices and local thermal
comfort criteria
Berlin: Beuth, 2006

Moisture

Marko Pinterić
Building Physics: From Physical Principles
to International Standards
New York: Springer, 2017

Horst Kuchling
Taschenbuch der Physik
20th edition. Munich: Carl Hanser, 2010

DIN EN 15193-1:2017-10
Energy performance of buildings –
Energy requirements for lighting –
Part 1: Specifications, Module M9
Berlin: Beuth, 2017

DIN 4108-3:2014-11
Wärmeschutz und
Energie-Einsparung in Gebäuden –
Teil 3: Klimabedingter Feuchteschutz –
Anforderungen, Berechnungsverfahren und
Hinweise für Planung und Ausführung
Berlin: Beuth Verlag, 2014

Wolfgang M. Willems, Kai Schild, Simone Dinter
Handbuch der Bauphysik
Wiesbaden: Vieweg Teubner, 2006, p. 5.24

Klaus W. Liersch, Normen Langner
Bauphysik kompakt: Wärme, Feuchte, Schall
3th edition. Berlin: Bauwerk Verlag, 2007

Jürgen Weber, Volker Hafkesbring
Bauwerksabdichtung in der Altbausanierung:
Verfahren und juristische Betrachtungsweise
2th edition. Wiesbaden: Springer Vieweg, 2008,
p. 42

Wolfgang M. Willems (ed.), Peter Häupl
Lehrbuch der Bauphysik: Schall – Wärme –
Feuchte – Licht – Brand – Klima
7th edition. Wiesbaden: Springer Vieweg, 2012

D. A. Rose
'Water movement in unsaturated
porous material', in: **RILEM Bulletin**
Paris, 16:29, 1965, pp. 119–123

Airtightness

DIN 1946-6:2009-05
Ventilation and air conditioning – Part 6:
Ventilation for residential buildings –
General requirements, requirements for
measuring, performance and labeling,
delivery/acceptance (certification) and
maintenance
Berlin: Beuth, 2009

Achim Bethe
Nutzungsdauertabellen für Wohngebäude:
Lebensdauer von Bau- und Anlagenteilen
Berlin: Beuth, 2010

DIN 4108-7:2011-01
Wärmeschutz und
Energie-Einsparung in Gebäuden –
Teil 7: Luftdichtheit von Gebäuden
Berlin: Beuth, 2011

Ole Fanger
Thermal Comfort
Danish Technical Press, 1970
(Reprint McGraw-Hill, New York, 1973)

Acoustics

Paul A. Tipler, Gene Mosca
Physics for Scientists and Engineers
6th edition. New York: W. H. Freeman, 2007

Ulf Hestermann, Ludwig Rongen,
Frick/Knöll Baukonstruktionslehre 1
Wiesbaden: Springer Vieweg, 2015

Richard Berger,
Über die Schalldurchlässigkeit, Dissertation,
Technical University Munich, 1911

Erich Schild, Hans Casselmann,
Günter Dahmen, Rainer Pohlenz
'Koinzidenzen – Grundüberlegungen',
in: **Bauphysik – Planung und Anwendung**
Braunschweig: Vieweg, 1977, p. 133

DIN 4109:2018-01
Sound insulation in buildings – Part 2:
Verification of compliance with the
requirements by calculation
Berlin: Beuth, 2018

Valery Rudnev, Don Loveless,
Raymond Cook, Micah Black,
'5.1.2 Frequency Choice and Power Density',
in: **Handbook of Induction Heating**
New York/Basel: Marcel Dekker, 2003,
pp. 227–228

Wolfgang M. Willems, Kai Schild, Diana Stricker
Schallschutz: Bauakustik. Grundlagen -
Luftschallschutz – Trittschallschutz
Wiesbaden: Springer Vieweg, 2012

Gottfried C. Lohmeyer, Heinz Bergmann,
Matthias Post, 'Schallschutz', in:
Praktische Bauphysik – Eine Einführung
mit Berechnungsbeispielen
5th edition. Wiesbaden: Teubner, 2005, p. 446

Light

DIN 5034-1:2011-07
Daylight in interiors –
Part 1: General requirements
Berlin: Beuth, 2011

DIN 5034-2:1985-02
Daylight in interiors –
Part 2: Fundamental principles
Berlin: Beuth, 1985

DIN 5034-3:2007-02
Daylight in interiors – Part 3: Calculation
Berlin: Beuth, 2007

DIN 5034-4:1994-09
Daylight in interiors – Part 4: Simplified
determination window sizes for dwellings
Berlin: Beuth, 1994

DIN 5034-5:2010-11
Daylight in interiors – Part 5: Measurement
Berlin: Beuth, 2010

DIN 5034-6:2007-02
Daylight in interiors – Part 6: Simplified
determination of suitable dimensions for
rooflights
Berlin: Beuth, 2007

DIN V 18599-4:2016-10
Energy efficiency of buildings – Calculation
of the net, final and primary energy demand
for heating, cooling, ventilation, domestic
hot water and lighting – Part 4: Net and final
energy demand for lighting
Berlin: Beuth, 2016

DIN EN 12464-1:2011-08
Light and lighting – Lighting of work places –
Part 1: Indoor work places
Berlin: Beuth, 2011

DIN EN 12464-2:2014-05
Light and lighting – Lighting of work places –
Part 2: Outdoor work places
Berlin: Beuth, 2014

Christoph Reinhart
Daylighting Handbook I: Fundamentals,
Designing with the Sun
www.DaylightingHandbook.com, 2014

Mohamed Boubekri
Daylighting Design: Planning Strategies
and Best Practice Solutions
Basel: Birkhäuser, 2014

Building Physics and Materials

Terri Meyer Boake
Understanding Steel Design: An Architectural
Design Manual
Basel: Birkhäuser, 2012

Michael Green, Jim Taggart
Tall Wood Buildings: Design, Construction and
Performance
Basel: Birkhäuser, 2017

Dirk E. Hebel, Felix Heisel
Cultivated Building Materials: Industrialized
Natural Resources for Architecture and
Construction
Basel: Birkhäuser, 2017

Martin Peck (ed.)
Modern Concrete Construction Manual
Munich: Edition Detail, 2014

Jan Wurm
Glass Structures: Design and Construction of
Self-Supporting Skins
Basel: Birkhäuser, 2007

Building Physics and the Envelope

Ulrich Knaack, Tillmann Klein,
Marcel Bilow, Thomas Auer
Façades: Principles of Construction
Second and revised edition
Basel: Birkhäuser, 2014

Maarten Meijs, Ulrich Knaack
Components and Connections:
Principles of Construction
Basel: Birkhäuser, 2009

Gerhard Hausladen, Michael de Saldanha,
Petra Liedl, Christina Sager
Climate Design: Solutions for Buildings
that Can Do More with Less Technology
Basel: Birkhäuser, 2005

Manfred Hegger, Volker Auch-Schwelk,
Matthias Fuchs, Thorsten Rosenkranz
Baustoff-Atlas
Munich: Edition Detail, 2005

Thomas Herzog, Roland Krippner, Werner Lang
Façade Construction Manual
Second revised and expanded edition
Munich: Edition Detail, 2017

Christian Schittich (ed.)
In Detail: Building Skins:
Concepts, Layers, Materials
Basel: Birkhäuser and Munich:
Edition Detail, 2001

Index

Illustration credits

Cover photograph: Ed White
(Wood Innovation and Design Centre, MGA |
Michael Green Architecture, Prince George, 2014)

1 Introduction
p. 6 Sascha Hickert (Selfridges Department Store,
Birmingham, Future Systems, 2003)
1 F. F. Peters

2 Thermal Energy
p. 12 Sascha Hickert (San Telmo Museum
Extension, San Sebastian, Nieto Sobejano
Arquitectos, 2011)

3 Moisture
p. 26 Sascha Hickert (Fabric Formwork, Carina
Kisker and Sascha Hickert, Technical University
Darmstadt, 2017)
1 Larissa Bewersdorff
2 Ingenieurbüro Stolze
5, 6, 7, 8 LIG BAU
10 Larissa Bewersdorff
12, 13, 14, 15, 16, 17 Ingenieurbüro Stolze
20 Drawing based on:
Wolfgang M. Willems, Peter Häupl, *Lehrbuch der
Bauphysik: Schall – Wärme – Feuchte – Licht –
Brand – Klima*, 7th edition. Wiesbaden: Springer
Vieweg, 2012, p. 206
27 Drawing based on:
Jürgen Weber, Volker Hafkesbring,
*Bauwerksabdichtung in der Altbausanierung:
Verfahren und juristische Betrachtungsweise*,
2th edition. Wiesbaden: Springer Vieweg, 2008,
p. 4

4 Airtightness
p. 44 Sascha Hickert (School of Economics
and Business, Pamplona, Juan M. Otxotorena
Arquitectos, 2012)
3 Drawing based on: Ole Fanger,
Thermal Comfort. Danish Technical Press, 1970
(Reprint McGraw-Hill, New York, 1973)
5, 7, 8, 9, 10, 11, 12, 13 Ingenieurbüro Langner

5 Acoustics
p. 56 Sascha Hickert (Rey Juan Carlos Hospital,
Madrid, Rafael de La-Hoz, 2012)
2, 3, 4 Drawing based on:
Wolfgang M. Willems, Kai Schild, Diana Stricker,
*Schallschutz: Bauakustik. Grundlagen –
Luftschallschutz – Trittschallschutz.*
Wiesbaden: Springer Vieweg, 2012
7 Drawing based on: DIN 4109-32: Schallschutz
im Hochbau – Teil 32: Daten für die rechnerischen
Nachweise des Schallschutzes (Bauteilkatalog) –
Massivbau. Berlin: Beuth, 2016
8 Drawing based on: ETH Zürich, Chair for
Building Physics
9, 10 Drawing based on:
Wolfgang M. Willems, Kai Schild, Diana Stricker,
*Schallschutz: Bauakustik. Grundlagen –
Luftschallschutz – Trittschallschutz.*
Wiesbaden: Springer Vieweg, 2012
15 Drawing based on: DIN 4109-32: Schallschutz
im Hochbau – Teil 32: Daten für die rechnerischen
Nachweise des Schallschutzes (Bauteilkatalog) –
Massivbau. Berlin: Beuth, 2016

6 Light
p. 74 Sascha Hickert (New Trade Fair Basel
Building, Basel, Herzog & de Meuron, 2013)

7 Building Physics in Practice
p. 92 Sascha Hickert (Franklin D. Roosevelt
Station Post Office, New York, Emery Roth & Sons
Architects, 1968)

8 Building Physics and Materials
p. 104 Sascha Hickert (Palacio Euskalduna,
Bilbao, Federico Soriano & Dolores Palacios
Arquitectos, 1999)
4, 7, 11, 14 Getty Images
18, 19, 20 from: Michael Green, Jim Taggart,
*Tall Wood Buildings: Design, Construction and
Performance*. Basel: Birkhäuser, 2017, p. 27, 28

9 Building Physics and the Building Envelope
p. 118 Sascha Hickert (Bauhaus Dessau –
Prellerhaus, Dessau, Louis Preller, 1926)
8, 9, 10 Tomislav Kovacevic
22 F. F. Peters

We are very grateful to these image providers.
All other illustrations were created specifically for
this book or were provided by the authors.